The Retirement Secret

The
RETIREMENT
SECRET

A Simple Approach to
Financial Peace-of-Mind

*Wishing you a retirement
full of Peace of Mind!*

Pat S

PAT STRUBBE

HOUNDSTOOTH
PRESS

THE RETIREMENT SECRET
A Simple Approach to Financial Peace-of-Mind

ISBN   978-1-5445-1914-2 *Hardcover*
       978-1-5445-1913-5 *Paperback*
       978-1-5445-1912-8 *Ebook*

For my beautiful wife, Janelle, because your love, support, and ability to gently help me stay focused on the most important things are all invaluable to me. Thank you for being my perfect partner in faith, marriage, and parenthood.

CONTENTS

PREFACE

I was six years old when the words that came out of my mouth shocked my mother. In fact, to this day, she says it was the most embarrassed she has ever been in her entire life!

We were standing in line in the lobby of our YMCA. From my six-year-old perspective, that line was a mile long!

Now, before I finish my story, let me tell you that when I would go to the store with my mom, I would sometimes ask her if I could have something. "Mommy, can I have this toy? Mommy, can I have this sugar-coated cereal?" My mom had a set answer to this question. Maybe your parents had the same set answer for you. If you have children, maybe you have YOUR set answer for them.

My mom's set answer never changed: "We can't afford it." Now, *could* we afford it? Yeah, probably.

But was it worth buying? In my mom's eyes, definitely not.

Now back to my story. My mom told me that we were going to

the YMCA to sign up for swim lessons. I was BEYOND excited! This was the day I had been waiting for!

I saw that long line and I didn't know if I could wait until we get to the front! Finally, we faced a woman sitting at a folding table collecting payments. She looked up at my mom and said, "That will be $3." I panicked, grabbed my mom's arm, and said:

"MOMMY, CAN WE AFFORD IT?"

At that moment, my mom felt like a million eyes were staring at her, and in her mind, she was worrying, *Do they think we are broke? Do they think we can't provide even $3 for swimming lessons?*

Although I enjoy sharing that story, it reflects the lessons that I learned from my parents about money over the years. Some of these lessons have helped me in life, while others have definitely caused me to struggle.

Growing up, we were a typical middle-class household. My dad worked for a trucking company, and my mom stayed home until my sister and I got older. My parents both grew up on corn farms in southern Indiana. All of my grandparents lived through the Great Depression, and their lessons stuck with my parents:

- Work hard.
- If you don't have enough money right now, then don't buy it.
- And if you don't need it, don't buy it.
- You don't want to borrow money from the bank or from anyone else. If you do, pay it back as fast as you can.

In fact, as an adult, I learned that although we were living on a tight budget when I was small, my parents were busy paying down their mortgage balance as quickly as they could. They learned that from their parents. Here I thought we were "just getting by." But in fact, my parents were working hard to get ahead.

When my grandfather returned from serving in World War II, my grandparents bought a house and a small farm. They paid it off as fast as they could.

Then they saved.

Every chance they could, they would buy more farmland. When I was little, I remember my grandpa always seemed happiest when we were just walking around his farm.

But I also watched my parents worry about money: they worried about debt. They worried about having enough. They worried about the future. They never had peace with their finances.

Now that I've been advising clients on retirement for more than twenty years, I've seen that my parents aren't alone. Money is one of the biggest causes of stress in America.

But I've learned that it doesn't have to be that way. In fact, I've learned a secret. It's simple, and yet I've seen it provide comfort, peace of mind, and understanding regarding topics that many find overwhelming.

That's why I had to write this book. That secret is described and explained in these pages. It is my hope and prayer that it provides you with comfort and peace as well.

INTRODUCTION

Close your eyes and picture this scene: You're lounging by the water. Let's assume it's the crystal-clear ocean with white-sand beaches. The weather is perfect. Family and friends—all of your favorite people—surround you. You have your favorite beverage in your hand. You have spent the day doing your favorite activities. A gentle breeze floats by. You smile and let out a sigh of contentment.

What is the perfect cap to the perfect day?

You've been offline all day. What could it hurt to take out your cell phone to quickly see what's going on in the world? You see that the market was down quite a bit today. That makes you curious to check your investments app; unfortunately, you find out that they were down, too.

You set your drink down, stand up, and walk away from your loved ones. Your money is important, so you need to attend to it, and after all, it's YOUR responsibility!

Does this sound crazy to you? It does to me, and I've been advising people about their money for my entire adult life.

Have you or someone you loved actually done something similar to this? If yes, have you ever wondered why?

Because we are addicted to our phones? Well, yes, we know that is often true, don't we? But it's more than that.

Is it because investing is fun and exciting? Well, yes, that can be true for some. But there's something else.

The real answer is something that you may have never thought about but is truly life changing. The real answer lies in the way retirement has changed in America over the last couple of generations.

Think about what retirement was like for your parents or even for your grandparents. It wasn't too long ago that someone could work their entire adult lives at the same job, collect their gold watch, then head home and live the rest of their life off their company pension and Social Security. For many, investments were the last thing on their mind—if they even owned any! And yet, they retired successfully and without worrying about running out of money.

Then in the 1970s and '80s, everything started to change. First, IRAs were created and then the 401(k). Soon after, the company pension began to disappear. Slowly and surely, the responsibility for your retirement has shifted onto your shoulders. This is why I call it the:

DO-IT-YOURSELF RETIREMENT SYSTEM

Think back to when you first entered the workforce after finishing school. Imagine if, during your first morning, your supervisor said this to you:

"Congratulations on your graduation, and welcome to being a grown-up! Oh, by the way, in addition to all the normal stuff like paying your bills, now is a good time to tell you that you also have another job that no one has probably told you about before. You see, you are actually going to be your very own pension manager. That's right, you, and only you, will be responsible for creating the pension income that you will live on after you retire. Here's a quick list of things you will want to keep in mind.

"First, figure out when you want to retire.

"Next, figure out how long you think you will live. Make sure to keep in mind the longevity you've seen in your family as well as all of the advances that are being made in extending life spans.

"Next, figure out how much income you will want. (Oh, don't forget to predict what inflation will be over the next forty-plus years.)

"Next, figure out how much money you will need by retirement to create that income.

"Next, figure out how much money you will need to save every pay period to accumulate that much money. Of course, you will need to know what you will earn on your money to do that. We suggest you become an expert on the stock market and economy to get a better idea because anytime your accounts lose money, that is your problem.

"Oh, please keep in mind that these assumptions won't work if you're ever laid off or if you have serious health problems or become disabled.

"Also, don't mess with this money if you ever get divorced, or buy a house, or put kids through college.

"Good luck!"

Is it any wonder why retiring successfully is so hard? The truth is that the do-it-yourself retirement system is a failure. It places all of the responsibility onto the individual while giving them no training or education on how to actually do the job.

Dr. William Bernstein has written extensively about investing, and I believe he is one of the best due to his unique perspective. He holds a PhD in chemistry and worked for many years as a neurologist. After retiring from the field, he obtained his pilot's license and began a career as a thought leader in the field of investing. I share all this because Dr. Bernstein will be quoted throughout this book.

First, from an interview in the September 2012 issue of *Money* magazine, he nicely sums up how difficult it can be to create a do-it-yourself retirement:

> I've flown airplanes, and as a doctor, I've taken care of kids who can't walk. Investing for retirement is probably harder than either of those first two activities, yet we expect people to be able to do it on their own.[1]

In addition to the difficulty, the timing for those planning their retirement may be as challenging as we've ever seen. The year

---

[1] George Mannes, "The Worst Retirement Investing Mistake? Advisor and Author William Bernstein Says It's Not Knowing When to Take Money off the Table," *Money*, September 2012.

2019 marked a ten-year-long run of the US economy growing. It's the longest in recorded history, which goes back to 1854![2]

Now add to that the incredible market and economic fallout from the coronavirus in 2020. The first quarter of the year was the worst first quarter in the history of the Dow Jones. That means it was the worst in more than 120 years. This crisis further proves just how fragile a do-it-yourself retirement really is.

The bottom line is that planning your retirement is hard, and it may be as difficult right now as it has been at any other time.

But thankfully, many years ago, I was introduced to an extremely simple idea that makes this do-it-yourself system far easier to understand. It reduces worry and gives people peace of mind. Rather than share it with you in something like a textbook, the following pages share a story—a story that started in my last book.

In my book *Save Your Retirement*, Dick and Jane are nearing retirement, and with the help of their friend Tommy, they meet the seven retirement villains. They introduce Dick and Jane to seven areas to plan for in retirement:

1. LADY LONGEVITY

Of course, we all want to live a long, healthy life, but Lady Longevity puts an evil spin on our wish. Her goal is to try to make you ignore the possibility of a long life in your retirement plan, thereby leaving you penniless and without choices if you outlive your money! Truly evil!

2   "Economy: Economic Growth and Economic Cycles." *Crestmont Research*, 3 Mar. 2014, https://www.crestmontresearch.com/economy/.

2. THE INVISIBLE ENEMY

This photo is of one of the rare occasions he allowed us to see him, because normally, he remains completely hidden. He is inflation, and his goal is to make things FAR more expensive the longer you live—ruining your retirement lifestyle!

3. EVIL UNCLE SAM

We all know that we need to pay taxes to the IRS, but Evil Uncle Sam goes a step further. He looks for all the different ways he can squeeze more and more money out of retirees. These taxes often don't affect the rich OR the poor. Instead, he goes after the people who work their whole lives to try to save for a comfortable retirement: you and me!

4. SARAH SELF-PAY

Sure, our government provides retirees with Medicare, but what about all the types of illnesses Medicare *don't* cover?

Nursing care can cost up to $7,000 a month or even more!

Sarah Self-Pay's goal is to force you to pay ALL of that out of your savings until there's nothing left!

5. ICEBERG IVAN

Ivan pulls the fees out of your savings and investments. Like the "tip of the iceberg," he tries to make sure you can't see them.

His goal is to cost you hundreds of thousands of dollars during your retirement, all the while keeping those fees hidden under the surface and out of sight!

6. SYSTEMATIC SAMMY

Sammy poses as a financial planner and gives you what sounds like a logical plan for you to take income systematically from your nest egg during your retirement.

Little do you suspect that his "plan" could destroy your nest egg faster than you can say "a wolf in sheep's clothing!"

7. ANTIQUATED ANDY

At first glance, Andy may seem harmless, but he represents outdated investment strategies that many Wall Street firms refuse to update. These strategies could expose your nest egg to many unnecessary risks. A true hazard to your *wealth*!

In the end, the Super Retirement Planner teaches Dick and Jane how to plan and work to protect themselves from all of these villains. We assumed they lived happily ever after.

In this book, we fast-forward eight years. Dick and Jane are indeed happily retired, and they meet some new friends: Jack and Jill. (What did you expect their names to be?)

Save Your Retirement! was designed to teach you about seven villains. Soon, you will be introduced to three more people. They will be Jack and Jill's mentors: Wall Street William, Safe Susan, and Endowment Edward.

In this story, I will share a secret that I have seen improve many lives, and it is my hope that it improves yours.

Chapter 1

═══

SEARCHING FOR THE SECRET

"It's time to recognize that your retirement security is in your hand alone."
—DAN KADLEC, "WHY YOUR 401K MATCH WILL GET CUT," *TIME*

"Jack! Hurry up. We don't want to be late!"

"Just a minute!" Jack shouted back down the stairs.

Jill went upstairs and walked into their bedroom. "What on earth is taking so long?"

Jack looked at Jill. "I just don't know what I want to wear."

Jill shook her head as they both laughed.

"In thirty-five years of marriage, I'm pretty sure you've never said that! But seriously, are you ready yet? I want to get going."

Jack pulled on a golf shirt and spent about three seconds pushing his hair around. "All right, I'm ready!"

"I'm sorry, honey," Jack said as they climbed into the car. "I didn't realize you wanted to get there so early. I'm not going to lie to you; I'm a little anxious about this get-together."

Jill was caught off guard by his comment and looked at him. "Really? What would be bothering you about it?"

Jack felt silly even talking about it. "I guess I feel like I'm a little old to be the new kid trying to make friends."

"Oh, come on, you like getting to know other people," Jill said with a smile. "Is that really all it is? We've had a crazy few months. Is it all finally catching up to you?"

"Maybe," Jack said while sitting at a stoplight.

Jill said, "Well, thank you for admitting it. It was only about four months ago that you got the transfer opportunity to move to the practice here."

Jack nodded as he started to accelerate. "Wow, that is kind of wild to think about. So much has happened since then."

"Exactly," Jill said. "Then we had to put our house on the market and sell it, bought our house and moved to Metropolis, and tried to figure out where everything is here.

"On top of all of that, you're working in a completely different practice with other surgeons you're still getting to know and with new patients. That is a lot to deal with."

Jack nodded again. "Oh, it definitely is a lot, but you know me. I can usually deal with stuff by just putting my head down and getting to work. I figured this would be the same."

Jill smiled. "Oh, I definitely know you! And you have done great. This is just so much more than we're used to. I don't know about you, but it has been a relief that we found our new church home. And I am excited about tonight's get-together. It will be fun to meet more people in the congregation. Hopefully, this will start feeling more like home."

As Jack pulled into their church parking lot, he said, "I'm happy we found this place, too. I guess I should look forward to tonight instead of pretending I'm going to a junior high dance!"

They shared a laugh at the comparison.

∗ ∗ ∗

Jack and Jill were the first ones to arrive, so they grabbed cups of ice water and sat down at a table. A few minutes later, a couple walked up to them, and the husband asked, "Are these seats taken?"

Jill quickly and energetically said, "They're all yours!" while waving at the seats next to them.

After they introduced themselves, Jack asked, "Dick, what kind of work do you do?"

"I was an engineer for thirty-eight years, but I'm happy to say that I'm retired now," Dick said with a smile.

Jack leaned forward with his eyebrows raised.

"Wow, you're already retired? That's great! If you don't mind me asking, you look so young. I'm curious about how old you are."

"Man, I wish people told me I looked young more often," Dick chuckled. "I'm sixty-three, but I should add that Jane is **much** younger than me. She's only sixty-one!"

"Well, that is really great," Jack replied. "I figured we were around the same age. We're both sixty, but of course, Jill is much younger than me, too!"

Over the course of the evening, they determined that all four of them enjoyed golfing, so they exchanged cell phone numbers and discussed possible dates to get together.

* * *

"See? I told you that you were good at making friends!" Jill teased Jack on their drive home.

"You were definitely right," Jack replied. "They seemed like really nice people, don't they?"

"Absolutely. I'm looking forward to getting to know them," Jill responded.

Once home, they settled on the couch with a glass of wine. It was quiet until Jill broke the silence.

"Honey, how could they be retired already? It sounded like they retired when they were around our age."

Jack pondered her question. "I have no idea. You know, I honestly wasn't giving retirement a ton of thought until recently. When both of us hit sixty, it kind of dawned on me that it is creeping up pretty fast. Don't get me wrong; I think we're doing pretty well with our savings and investments, but I'm not entirely sure if we're doing everything exactly right."

Jill leaned in. "You mean to tell me that in addition to all the other craziness in our lives the past three or four months that you've been worrying about retirement, too?"

"Okay, honey, calm down," Jack assured her. "You don't need to be my therapist right now. It's not like this was some master plan that I had to worry about myself. I just mean that it has started to pop into my mind more. I just wonder about it at random times. Keep in mind, sometimes I think about it a lot more than at other times. Like not that long ago, the stock market dropped about 15 percent in a couple of weeks. I can't help but look up the value of our accounts, then start worrying about whether they will come back up in time for us to retire."

"I wasn't trying to put you on my therapist's couch," Jill said. "It's probably overdue that we talk about this. How *do* we actually retire? I mean, in addition to all the things we want to do, just the two of us, and I've been talking with the kids about doing things with them and the grandkids.

"I know that we've worked hard. I know that we've saved money. I know that you've done a good job with our investments. But how do we take all of that and live off it? And how do we make sure we never run out of money?"

Jack smiled. "I think we're going to need more wine!"

They shared a laugh, then Jack continued.

"The truth is that I don't know the answer. I agree we've done a great job of saving and investing. Now we need to figure out how to turn all of that into a retirement. Since I'm sure you're going to ask, I do have concerns about it. We've worked and saved for so long. I don't want it all to be for nothing. We've known people who died in their sixties. They never even got to enjoy retirement!

"I don't want to work forever, and I know you don't either. So I've just been thinking more about making sure we're on track to retire sooner rather than later so we can enjoy retirement together."

Jill leaned forward to give Jack a hug and a kiss. "Thank you, dear. I feel the same way. It is scary when people you know pass away. And you can't help but think about yourself. By the way, I hope you know that I didn't expect you to have all of those answers. They're just things I've been wondering."

"Me, too!" Jack quickly replied.

Jill thought for a minute.

"What if we ask Dick and Jane how they retired?"

Jack held up his wineglass. "Now, *that* is a great idea!"

* * *

Two weeks later, the two couples golfed together and shared lunch at the clubhouse. Toward the end of the meal, Jack said, "Hey, do you all mind if I ask you a personal question?

"How did you guys retire? I mean, did you do it all by yourselves? Did you have some kind of advisor you worked with? You both seem so calm and content. It's difficult for us to even imagine feeling that way."

"I'm actually so glad you asked," Dick replied with a smile.

"I was going to ask you today if you had anyone locally to help you with your finances."

"No, not locally, and honestly not ever," Jack replied. "We've socked money away into retirement plans ourselves for years. But we've been talking about trying to figure out what's next, and then when I see the stock market drop 15 percent so quickly, it makes me anxious."

Dick and Jane smiled at each other knowingly.

"Okay, what is that look about?" Jill asked.

Jane laughed. "Oh, I just know that this is one of his favorite things to do. So that was my 'Here we go again!' look."

"She's absolutely right. This *is* one of my favorite things to do," Dick said. "The truth is, I was *way* too confident that I knew what I was doing for our retirement. Then we met our retirement planner. He helped us understand everything we needed to do. Trust me; his team is the best. In fact, you probably won't believe what will happen to you."

"What does *that* mean?" Jill replied.

Dick smiled. "I'll tell you what. I'll call today and ask them to schedule a meeting with you. Trust us. Between now and your meeting, your life will be completely changed!"

Jack and Jill were still wondering what Dick was talking about, and their faces showed it.

Jane saw this, leaned in, and said, "Trust us."

* * *

Dick called Super Retirement Planner's office and left a voice mail. On Monday morning, the office called Jack and Jill to schedule a meeting for two weeks later.

Over the course of the two weeks, and with the help of Dick and Jane, Jack and Jill met all seven retirement villains. They learned all about how these villains can harm you during your retirement. Just as importantly, they also learned the ways to protect themselves from the villains.

Then it was time to finally meet Super Retirement Planner. They had never been more excited about a meeting!

* * *

When Jack, Jill, and Super Retirement Planner met, Jack opened the discussion with, "So Dick has told me that you had the 'retirement secret.' We're ready for it!"

Super Retirement Planner smiled. "Since you're friends with Dick and Jane, we'll make an exception. Before revealing the secret, I have a lesson that is the foundation of all financial planning. The world of finance and investing is obsessed with ideas such as tips, tactics, and strategies. But none of those should be considered or implemented without first understanding principles. The problem is that it is our human nature to get excited about the next big thing. We call those the 'new, shiny objects.'"

"Honey, it sounds like he already knows you!" Jill said.

Jack chuckled. "Guilty as charged."

"He's definitely not alone," Super Retirement Planner continued. "Before we get to specific tactics and strategies, we know it's far more beneficial that you understand the principles. There are three timeless principles of investing that everyone needs to know. How does that sound?"

Jill opened up her notepad. "We're ready!"

Chapter 2

===

WHAT IS THE "PERFECT" INVESTMENT?

Super Retirement Planner let out a belly laugh.

"Okay, sounds good! I'll start by asking you, if you were able to design the absolute perfect investment where you could put all of your money, how would you describe that perfect investment?"

Now it was Jack's turn to laugh.

"That's easy," he said. "It would make *a lot* of money!"

Super Retirement Planner stood at the whiteboard in the conference room. "Yes, of course, we all want a high return on our money, right?"

While he wrote **High Return** on the whiteboard, he asked, "What else would you like this investment to do for you?"

This time, Jack and Jill contemplated the question. After a few moments, Jill responded, "Well, we would want our money to be safe so we know we couldn't lose it."

Super Retirement Planner wrote **Completely Safe.**

"Yes. Allow me to use the definition I think most people think of: what we're referring to here is that the value of your account can never go down. Does that sound good?"

Jack and Jill responded, "YES!" in unison.

"Great," Super Retirement Planner said. "Okay, now, how else would you describe this perfect investment?"

This time, Jack and Jill both sat quietly for a little while.

Finally, Jack said, "High return and safe already sounds like the perfect investment. What more would we want?"

"Don't worry, this is the toughest one to figure out," Super Retirement Planner responded. "Let me throw out a number. Would you consider 10 percent a year to be a good return?"

Jack and Jill both nodded approvingly.

"Super," Super Retirement Planner continued. "So now we find you a hypothetical account that offers you 10 percent per year guaranteed, and your account is completely safe. Sounds great, right? Or maybe perfect?"

Jack and Jill sensed that there was a catch they had missed.

Then Super Retirement Planner added, "There's only one problem: this so-called perfect investment is a lifetime contract. So you are earning 10 percent per year. But you can't touch your money—ever! That doesn't do you a lot of good now, does it?"

"Ah, yes! It would also need to be liquid!" Jack said.

"You've got it. For an investment to be perfect, you have to be able to access it anytime you want without any penalties," Super Retirement Planner replied.

He wrote **Access** on the whiteboard.

"Now, I have great news for you. You see, there is a name for an investment that offers high returns, safety, and total access. Do either of you know what it is?"

Jack and Jill both leaned in out of anticipation.

Jill's pen hovered over her notepad. "No, what is it?"

"It is a **dream!**"

All three of them shared a good laugh.

"Now, I didn't go through that exercise just to tell that joke. I wanted to make sure you could always remember that the first timeless principle of investing is to **always remember that there is no such thing as a perfect investment**, and no account can give you all three of these characteristics. Does that make sense?"

Jack and Jill nodded.

"Great," Super Retirement Planner said. "This simple truth can save you a great deal of heartache. Are both of you familiar with Bernie Madoff?"

"Yeah, he's the guy who ripped people off, right?" Jack said.

"Yes, that's right," Super Retirement Planner responded. "Interestingly, he didn't promise anything crazy like doubling your money overnight. Wikipedia reports that what he promised were unusually consistent returns of around 10 percent per year and that you could withdraw money whenever you wanted. That sounds like a dream, doesn't it?"

Jack and Jill again nodded.

"So the first lesson here is to protect yourselves. Simply put, if it sounds too good to be true, it either IS too good to be true, or you just haven't heard the bad news yet!

"This can help save you from big losses. But it can also help you protect your sanity. There is no doubt that at some time, you'll be chatting with friends or family, and someone will be bragging about how great their investments are doing. And you'll be tempted to think, *Hmm, do they know something I don't know?* Now you know that there is no way for someone else to have a perfect investment either!"

"Oh yeah, the guys at the club love to brag about how great their investments are," Jack said. "That makes total sense!"

"Perfect," said Super Retirement Planner. "The second lesson here is that it's important to have reasonable expectations for each of your accounts. It's unfair to expect any of them to be perfect."

Super Retirement Planner paused.

"If that makes sense, let's jump into the next important point to take away here. Although it is unreasonable to expect any investment to offer all three of these characteristics, it is absolutely possible for one investment to offer two of the three. Let's go through them. Look at 'Safe' and 'Access.' Can you think of an account that keeps your money safe and lets you take money out of it whenever you want?"

This time, Jill jumped in first. "Sure. How about a checking account?"

"That's exactly right," Super Retirement Planner said. "Your checking account is safe. It lets you draw your money out when you want it. But you definitely don't put money there expecting a big return, right?"

Jack and Jill nodded again.

"Okay, that was the easiest one," Super Retirement Planner said. "Let's now move to these two: 'Safe' and 'High Return.' Think of somewhere that does not give you access to your money anytime but gives you a better return than your checking account. You may not think the return is 'high,' so to speak, but it is a higher return than the checking account."

Jack and Jill looked at each other, and Jill said with very little confidence, "Would that be a CD?"

Super Retirement Planner smiled. "Yes! That's right! With a certificate of deposit, you give up access, and in exchange, you get a better return! Well done!

"Okay, let's move on to the last one: this time, we give up 'Safety.' So now you have complete access to your money, and you have a high return. In this example, I will say that what I'm thinking of gives you either a higher average return over time or gives you the potential for higher average returns."

Jack looked very unsure but ventured, "I guess that sounds like the stock market to me."

"Yes, you all nailed all of them. Great job! Since we're talking about investment options, I would use the example of a stock mutual fund here. It definitely would not be considered safe, but the fund would generally give you access to get your money because you can sell it any day the market is open. Even though we don't know exactly what type of return you would get, historical averages would suggest that a stock mutual fund would at least give us the opportunity for higher returns. Does all of that make sense?"

Jack and Jill nodded again, so he kept going.

"Let me move right into our next timeless lesson: would you ever want your entire life savings to be in your checking account, or in a CD, or in stock mutual funds?"

Jack and Jill both exclaimed, "No!"

"Correct. Now let me ask a tougher question: Why?"

This time, neither Jack nor Jill responded as quickly.

"Well, if it were all in our checking account, we wouldn't be getting any higher returns, and if it were all in a CD, we wouldn't have any access without penalties, and if it were all in stock mutual funds, we wouldn't have any guarantee that we wouldn't lose money," Jill said.

Super Retirement Planner paused, then said, "A+! That is the exact right answer!

"What you have just described is why it is so important that we all diversify our money. Or, in plain simple terms, we never want to put all our eggs in one basket.

"Now I have one final point I would like to make before we move to the next topic. It is helpful to remember that based on everything we just covered, wherever we decide to place your nest egg, keep in mind that since there is no perfect investment, every single account will have at least one characteristic you don't like!"

Jack smiled and said, "Well, that's kind of a bummer."

Super Retirement Planner laughed.

"Yes, I suppose it is," he replied. "But I would rather you know this truth now rather than to be disappointed later. Our goal will be to find a mixture of investments that complement one another. Hopefully, that means that in the end, the characteristics you don't like won't bother you all that much."

Jack responded, "Now, *that* sounds better!"

"Okay, are you ready for the next timeless truth?" Super Retirement Planner asked.

"I'm excited to hear it!" Jack said.

SUMMARY OF MAJOR POINTS

- There is no such thing as a perfect investment.
- If it sounds too good to be true, it probably is.
- Of the three main investment characteristics, some options can provide you with two of the three.
- Never put all your eggs into one basket.
- It helps to keep perspective and remember that no matter how "good" an investment is, there will have to be at least one characteristic about it that you won't like.

Chapter 3

WHAT IS THE PURPOSE OF YOUR MONEY?

"If you're an inch off on landing, no big deal. If you're an inch off on takeoff, you miss the moon by a million miles."

—NEIL ARMSTRONG, *ESPN* MAGAZINE, JULY 2019

After a quick refreshment break, everyone settled in around the table again. Super Retirement Planner started.

"Okay, Jack seems like he's raring to go! Let's jump into the second timeless principle of investing. When we're done, you're going to understand why most financial advisors and the financial media have it all wrong."

Jack and Jill looked surprised. Jill said, "That's a bold statement, and you've got my attention!"

"Great," started Super Retirement Planner. "First, I need to get a little technical. There is a financial concept published in 1952, and it has become the basis of personal finance. Let me read this quick summary to you from Investopedia. It's very technical, but it's an important place to start:

> Modern portfolio theory (MPT) is a theory on how risk-averse investors can construct portfolios to optimize or maximize expected return based on a given level of market risk, emphasizing that risk is an inherent part of higher reward. According to the theory, it's possible to construct an "efficient frontier" of optimal portfolios offering the maximum possible expected return for a given level of risk. This theory was pioneered by Harry Markowitz in his paper "Portfolio Selection," published in 1952 by the Journal of Finance. He was later awarded a Nobel Prize for developing the MPT.

"Okay, I know there is a lot of jargon in there, so let me translate," Super Retirement Planner continued. "Mr. Markowitz used math to show how for each level of risk an investor takes, there is a corresponding amount of return. In other words, if you're going to invest all of your money in more aggressive investments like the stock market, over time, you should expect to earn a better return. However, if you keep all of your money in guaranteed bank accounts, you expect a lower return."[3]

---

3   Sharma, Asankhaya. "Build a Portfolio of Cryptocurrencies Using Modern Portfolio Theory." *Medium*, Medium, 2 Dec. 2017, https://medium.com/@asankhaya/build-a-portfolio-of-cryptocurrencies-using-modern-portfolio-theory-d65217858660.

An Efficient Frontier
The Power of Diversification

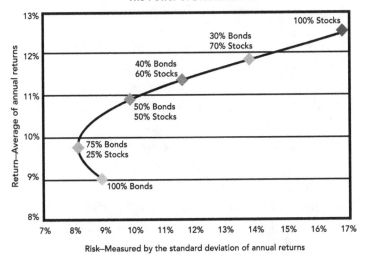

Risk—Measured by the standard deviation of annual returns

"Higher risk, higher return. Lower risk, lower return. The guy gets a Nobel Prize for *that*?" Jack asked.

"Well, there's a little more to it than that," Super Retirement Planner said. "This chart of the efficient frontier was revolutionary. It gave investors an idea of what type of risk and return they might be able to expect over time, depending on the mixture of stocks and bonds in their portfolio. Check out the lowest two points for something interesting. Markowitz showed that having 25 percent stocks and 75 percent bonds was less risky than having all your money in bonds. Even though this is initially odd to most of us, it is a simple example of why diversification is so valuable!"

"Yes, that's actually quite interesting," Jill added. "Logic tells you that the less you would have in the stock market, the lower the risk and the lower the returns."

"Yes, you're right," Super Retirement Planner agreed. "It's just one little example of why divvying up your money into different types of investments can be very powerful."

"There is a common expression used in the financial services industry, and it refers to a 60/40 portfolio," Super Retirement Planner continued. "Generally, that means that someone has 60 percent of their portfolio in the stock market and 40 percent in the bond market. Many in our industry, not to mention the financial media, believe 60/40 is the 'optimal' portfolio for investors. The reason they hold to this belief is because of this chart. As you can see, 60 percent in stocks provides a higher expected return than portfolios with fewer stocks. But when you move to 70 percent stocks or more, the risk level starts going up quickly.

"From this chart and a quick explanation, can you see why so many people think that a 60/40 portfolio is the best?"

"Yes, it does make sense," Jill said. "But something tells me that you aren't finished yet."

"Ah, Jill, you are catching on quite quickly! You're right that there is more to the story. In fact, I might even say that the people who believe this are completely wrong!"

"Wow, okay, you are fired up about this," Jack replied. "I can't wait to hear why."

"Gladly," Super Retirement Planner said. "Here is the next timeless principle: When you are investing, success isn't actually measured by who earns the highest rate of return. Success is measured by who accomplishes their goals. Before you determine where you put your money, you need to have a clear idea of what you want your money to do for you."

> INVESTING SUCCESS IS NOT MEASURED
> BY RATE OF RETURN. IT'S MEASURED BY
> HOW YOU ACCOMPLISH YOUR GOALS.

"If your goals are completely different than someone else's, logic dictates that you should use different strategies. For example, think about if we were trying to determine the 'best' mode of transportation. If I am going over to my next-door neighbor's home, how am I going to get there? I suppose I could drive, but I am pretty sure that I will just walk.

"If I'm going downtown for a date with my wife, I could walk, but it would take hours. We would be exhausted and probably sweaty, too! So, therefore, I will drive.

"If I'm going to go visit my old college friend in Los Angeles, it would be possible to drive, but it would take days. So I will likely fly. Do any of these examples mean that walking, driving, or flying are inherently 'better' than the other choices? Of course not. What determines my method of travel is my destination. Your investments are no different. If your goals are different than someone else's, then the 'best' mix of investments for you is going to be different than theirs."

"Yes, it definitely makes sense to me," Jack interjected. "But if you make the highest average return, wouldn't you automatically accomplish your goals?"

"That's a great question," Super Retirement Planner replied. "Sometimes, yes. Sometimes, no.

"Let's take an extremely oversimplified example to make this point. Let's take a hypothetical person who starts putting money into their 401(k) at age twenty-five, works until sixty-five, then lives off their nest egg until ninety-five. Let's assume that they averaged 8 percent returns per year. Does that sound reasonable?"

"Sure," Jack replied.

"Okay, great," said Super Retirement Planner. "Now let's assume that this investor's luck was the worst. In the first ten years of investing, the markets soared. Let's assume it was the same as the 1990s. During that decade, the S&P 500 went up an average of an incredible 19 percent per year!"[4]

"Holy smokes," said Jack, "I wish I made that much!"

"You bet!" said Super Retirement Planner. "Those gains helped this investor build a great nest egg. But of course, everything averages out in the end. You see, the worst ten-year stretch of investing for him came right when he turned sixty-five. Now, can you guess why that was the worst time for him?"

Jill jumped in. "Well, for one thing, this investor is older and therefore has less time to make the losses back."

"Exactly right," said Super Retirement Planner. "What else?"

"Well, not only do they not have time to make the money back, but if it happens at their retirement, then they can't earn the money back either," Jack said.

---

4   "Compound Annual Growth Rate (Annualized Return)." *CAGR of the Stock Market: Annualized Returns of the S&P 500*, http://www.moneychimp.com/features/market_cagr. htm.

"Also exactly right," said Super Retirement Planner. "There are two other reasons. Can one of you guess either of them?"

At first, Jack and Jill were stumped. Then Jill got an excited look on her face and shouted, "Systematic Sammy!"

Jack was a little bit startled but chuckled. "Aw, honey, nicely done. I should have thought of that!"

"Exactly right," said Super Retirement Planner. "When the balance of the investment account is being reduced by market losses at the same time as someone is withdrawing for retirement, it is a perfect storm that can accelerate the nest egg toward a zero balance.

"There is one final reason. This is the time when the investor has the most money to lose! In the first year of investing, the gain might have been 19 percent. But a 19 percent gain on $1,000 is $190. Better than nothing but not that big of a deal when you consider a lifetime of investing.

"What if this investor retired at sixty-five with $2 million to live off? Then a drop like late 2007 through early 2009 happened when the markets dropped in half. In that case, this investor could lose $1 million or more, and that's not even taking into account the effects of Systematic Sammy.

"That was an extreme example, but it shows how someone can earn a great average rate of return and still not accomplish their goals. Now are you comfortable retiring and basing your entire retirement income strategy on hoping that the markets provide you with average or better returns?"

"No," Jack and Jill said in unison.

"That," said Super Retirement Planner, "is what we mean about determining the purpose of your money. So what you've just told me is that the purpose of your money is not to earn the highest average return. It is to create an income for the rest of your life that you can count on.

"Here's an interesting example. One of my favorite authors, Dr. William Bernstein, put it this way in *Rational Expectations.*"

> The purpose of investing is not to simply optimize returns and make yourself rich. The purpose is to not die poor.

"Yes, that's exactly what we want," said Jill. "You're saying that people who talk about investing in newspapers, magazines, and TV shows are all focusing on the wrong thing. They are focused on the return instead of what we really want, which is to be able to retire comfortably."

Super Retirement Planner smiled.

"That is perfectly said, Jill. Our human nature always wants to seek out the biggest return whenever possible. So even when we *know* we should be focused on our goals, when we see an ad for something that's supposed to be so great, or when we hear someone else talking about investments, it's easy to lose our focus. Hopefully, you will remember this when those times come up."

"I think what you mean to say is, the next time one of Jack's buddies tells us about the investment opportunity of a lifetime, I can remind him of this conversation!" Jill said.

They all shared a big laugh.

"Okay, great," Super Retirement Planner said. "Before we move on, I want to introduce you to a man named Wade Pfau, PhD. He is a guy whom successful retirees owe a debt of gratitude to, yet I'm sure almost none of them have ever heard of him. He may be the leading expert on retirement strategies in the United States. Let me read to you what Dr. Pfau wrote about this topic in his book *How Much Can I Spend in Retirement?*" He opened the book and read.

> In 1991, Nobel laureate and MPT founder Harry Markowitz wrote in the first issue of Financial Services Review about how MPT was never meant to apply to the investment problems of a household. Rather, it was for large institutions with indefinite lifespans and no specific spending objectives for the portfolio. This should have been a eureka moment for the entire retirement income industry, but MPT is still misapplied today. The goal is to have cash flows available to meet spending needs as required, and investments are chosen in a way that meets those needs.

"Dr. Pfau is talking about using your nest egg to create income in retirement. He's talking about what people are trying to accomplish with their retirement savings: preserving it as long as possible, generating income to live off, and doing both for an unknown length of time.

"In other words, Markowitz himself told the financial industry that they misunderstood the entire point of his research, and no one listened! This is because the industry is built on selling to investors seeking the highest possible average return. Sadly, this means that as a whole, the industry does not care about helping people accomplish their goals."

"This seems so obvious now," Jack starts. "But we've been like everyone else and have always looked at everything the wrong way. It's crazy the way people talk about and think about investing and retirement. So is there any more to this point, or can we learn the last timeless principle now?"

Super Retirement Planner laughed.

"Jack, you're always ready for what's next! I love it! Yes, I think that covers this point. Do either of you need a break?"

Jack and Jill smiled, looked at each other, and shook their heads.

Super Retirement Planner said, "All right, let's do it!"

SUMMARY OF MAJOR POINTS

- The term *modern portfolio theory* (MPT) refers to the concept of creating "optimal" portfolios in an effort to generate "maximum" return for a given level of risk.
- But investors are not seeking to maximize the year-to-year rate of return. They are seeking to have cash flow available to meet their spending needs.
- Therefore, investing success is not measured in rate of return. It's measured by how you accomplish your goals.
- Investment decisions should start with determining what the purpose of your money is.

Chapter 4

___

WHICH PHASE ARE YOU IN?

"The longer I live, the more beautiful life becomes."

—FRANK LLOYD WRIGHT

"We've covered the fact that there's no perfect investment and that the purpose of your money needs to dictate what you do with it," Super Retirement Planner said. "The third timeless principle of investing is closely related to the second.

> The purpose of your money is affected the most by the phase of your investing lifetime you currently reside in.

"You see, although the 'retirement secret' is universal, it's important to understand that it applies to everyone differently depending on their circumstances.

"When you stop and think about our investing lifetime, climbing a mountain is a fitting analogy. Even though most of us aren't mountain climbers, we can visualize that climber when they have scaled one of the biggest mountains in the world. Picture someone at the top of Mount Everest."

"Ah, but wait," Super Retirement Planner continued. "Yes, they had a goal to scale Mount Everest, but when you think about it, their real goal was to scale Mount Everest *and* return safely back down to the bottom. So they have only really accomplished half of their goal!"

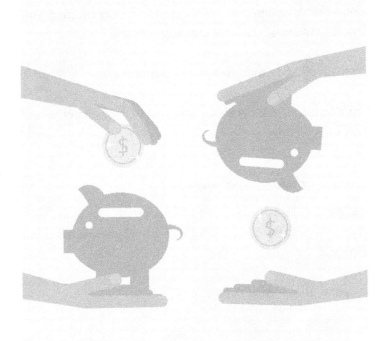

"Scaling up the mountain represents that portion of our investing lifetime when we are accumulating our nest egg. That moment of exhilaration at the top of the mountain represents the very moment of our retirement, and yes, we should absolutely celebrate that day!

"But we also shouldn't think that all of the work is over. We still need to get you down that mountain safely! You still have to make investment decisions about your nest egg, but now most retirees are also taking income from their investments, which changes their purpose dramatically.

"Although there are many factors that help you determine the purpose of your money, whether you are on your way up or down the mountain is one of the biggest factors affecting your investment decisions. Does that make sense?"

"Yes," Jill offered, "that analogy makes perfect sense."

"Wonderful. So let's quickly dig into each of these phases of your investing lifetime."

THE FIRST INVESTING PHASE

"Let me start by asking you to think back to the day each of you started your first full-time job after you had completed school. How old were you?"

Jack and Jill smiled at the memory.

"We were both twenty-two," Jack said.

"And what was going on in your lives?" Super Retirement Planner asked. "How were you dealing with money?"

Jill jumped in. "We were just trying to figure everything out. How were we going to pay our bills? How would we make the money last? How would we afford to buy our first house? How could we ever afford to have kids? The questions just went on and on."

"That is a process we all go through." Super Retirement Planner smiled. "I imagine retirement wasn't the biggest thing you were thinking about or worrying about."

"No, definitely not," Jack said. "Although I remember my dad telling me I should get started when I was young."

"Okay, great," Super Retirement Planner responded. "So let's imagine we could travel back to that time. You've just started working. Let me quickly take you through what we would have probably been talking about.

"First things first, we want everyone to have an emergency reserve. You would set aside some money in case your car breaks down and stick that money in the bank.

"Second, we would talk about any debt you might have had at that time and would have created a plan for how to pay that debt down as quickly as possible.

"Third, you mentioned your first home. I'm sure we would have talked about saving up for your down payment.

"Fourth and finally, we would have discussed retirement. So we would have talked about starting to begin building your retirement savings—no matter how small that might have been.

"Now, I'm sure you noticed this, but the entire process I just went through was using the last timeless principle: focusing on the purpose of the money to determine what to do next."

Jack and Jill nodded in agreement.

"Great!" Super Retirement Planner appreciated when his students were eager learners and followed along.

"So focusing on retirement, with regard to your twenty-two-year-old selves, the first goal is simply to get you started. This could have been putting a little into a company 401(k) each pay period if that was an option. Or putting a little every month into a mutual fund. It is important to create the habit of *something* going toward retirement regularly.

"The second thing is, if you're twenty-two and you're putting money into an account for retirement, that means that you probably weren't expecting to use that money for at least thirty-five or forty-five years. So what's the best advice for such a long-term strategy?"

Jill started to answer slowly. "Since it's supposed to be sitting there for decades, it seems like you would want it to be invested for the highest possible return."

"That's a very good answer and almost exactly right."

Jill laughed. "Hey, I'm happy to be close!"

"I would adjust your answer slightly," Super Retirement Planner responded. "We want it to be invested for the highest possible return and in an investment that you can stomach!

"You see, it doesn't matter if something averages 10 or 15 percent per year if it is so volatile that you panic and sell it the first time its value crashes. We call this our 'blinders strategy.'"

"When you have decades ahead of you," Super Retirement Planner explained, "the best thing you can do is start the habit of saving, then *leave it alone*! Even if you had online access back when you were twenty-two, there would have been no benefit for you to check your account balance every day, right?"

"Oh my goodness, he might have gone insane!" Jill said.

Jack grinned. "Yeah, you're probably right."

"Exactly," Super Retirement Planner said. "So the strategy for someone young saving for far into the future is simple: save, invest for growth, and leave it alone. That's it."

THE LAST INVESTING PHASE

"Now let's look into the future. You've announced your retirement. They've thrown a party for you, and you're leaving work for the last time. It feels exhilarating, right?"

"We both enjoy what we do, but we also look forward to the day when we don't have that work stress anymore," Jill said. "I think Jack *really* feels that way, even more than I do!"

Jack smiled and nodded in agreement.

Super Retirement Planner enjoyed watching Jack and Jill visualize that moment of successfully retiring.

"All right, so now you're retired. Your investment goals have completely changed, right?

"We were just talking about investing aggressively over the decades. But now, you want to preserve as much of your nest egg as possible, and you want to be able to generate the most income possible to support your retirement lifestyle.

"Let me ask you this: Do you think it would be wise for you to have all of your money in the stock market and ignore it? I suppose you could try withdrawing money monthly after you retire and hope that the money never runs out."

Jack jumped in right away. "Okay, now *that* would drive me insane!"

"As you get closer and closer to retirement, the stakes get higher and higher," Super Retirement Planner responded.

"In fact, the moment in which your financial life is at most risk is often the very date of your retirement."[5]

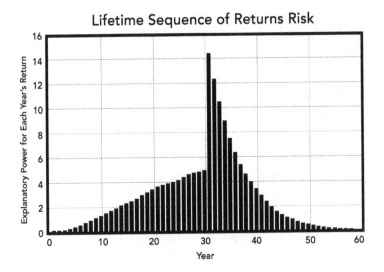

Lifetime Sequence of Returns Risk

"In this example," Super Retirement Planner pointed. "Dr. Pfau assumes someone begins saving for retirement at age thirty-five, retires at sixty-five, and lives until ninety-five. He also assumes this investor has a balanced portfolio of stocks and bonds throughout their investing lifetime. This chart represents the likelihood of someone going broke if the stock market sees a significant downturn at that point in their life.

"As you can see, that risk is extremely low at both thirty-five and ninety-five and skyrockets at sixty-five. Can either of you guess why the risk is so low at age thirty-five?"

"Yes," Jill responded. "When you've started investing, you not

---

5   https://io.wp.com/retirementresearcher.com/wp-content/uploads/2013/09/lifetime_sor-300x1711.jpg.

only have tons of time to recover, but you also don't have very much money invested, so your loss is smaller."

"Very good," Super Retirement Planner said. "Even if the percentage loss is huge, the loss in dollars is small. Now, how about why is the risk so low at age ninety-five?"

"Well, I guess it's because you're literally at the end of your life," Jack said.

"You got it. It's a lot tougher to run out of money when you're almost out of time, right? Now for the point that is critical to understand: the risk is the highest at the exact moment of retirement. And as we touched on before, this is due to a number of reasons." He then went on to list them out.

- You are no longer making and saving more money.
- You have the most money at risk of loss.
- And in this example, you still have thirty years ahead of you.

"So it is the perfect storm!" he said.

Jill looked shaken. "Wow, when you look at your retirement date in that chart, it is really scary."

Super Retirement Planner replied, "It *is* scary, which is why this type of planning is so incredibly valuable. This is how Dr. Pfau summarizes it.

> The financial market returns experienced near your retirement date matter a great deal more than you may realize. Retiring at the beginning of a bear market is incredibly dangerous. The average market return over a thirty-year period could be quite generous,

but if you experience negative returns in the early stages when you have started spending from your portfolio withdrawals can deplete wealth rapidly.

"The term that is sometimes used for this is peak vulnerability," Super Retirement Planner further explained. "Your anticipated future earnings are zero, your nest egg is likely at the biggest risk of your lifetime, and you have an unknown but potentially very long time frame ahead of you that requires income to support.

"Hopefully, you can see that how you invest in retirement is incredibly important!"

Jack and Jill nodded in approval.

Super Retirement Planner kept pushing forward. "Okay, good. Now, we did skip over one final extremely valuable point. This is one that may be particularly relevant to you."

THE MIDDLE INVESTING PHASE

"We know that someone younger with decades to invest should be as aggressive as they can handle. We know that someone at retirement age needs to protect themselves from large losses. But when and how do you make this huge switch from trying to accumulate as much money as possible to shifting to preserving that money and creating income with it?

"Let's look to author Dr. Bernstein's book *The Ages of the Investor*, who says it so well."

The trickiest and riskiest part of the process is the transition from the first to the second phase of investing.

Super Retirement Planner continued, "This makes sense. When you start putting your first few dollars into your 401(k), your investment strategy is more straightforward. When you're fully retired, your goals and the purpose of your money is quite clear. But how does someone make that switch?

"This is rarely talked about. Some people start shifting money five, ten, or fifteen years before their target retirement date. I've had other people tell me that weeks before they retired, they shifted their entire nest egg from stocks and bonds over to cash!

"Now, the point here isn't that there is some special formula or the perfect way to do this. The point here is that the years before your retirement are indeed critical, and it is important to be making your investment decisions based on where you are in your investing life span. Does that make sense?"

"Yes!" exclaimed Jack. "This is obviously the phase we're in right now, and we have no idea what we're supposed to do!"

Super Retirement Planner nodded.

"Jack, I completely understand because we meet people every single week who are trying to figure all of this out. Our industry has done a terrible job of explaining this to anyone.

"There is one concept that Dr. Bernstein has written about that I would like to close with, and that is the idea of 'winning the game.' You see, most of us spend our whole lives saving and investing, and for what? Ultimately, it's to have enough to take that leap and tell our bosses that we are choosing to stop working. Think of these decades of saving and investing as 'The

Game.' Now, once you've accumulated enough to make the decision to retire, you've actually 'won' the game, right?'"

"Yep!" said Jack. "That's definitely the goal!"

"Absolutely, but the weird thing is, a lot of people who have won the game do something that is completely illogical: they keep playing!

"Every year, thousands of baby boomers reach the point of winning the game, yet they leave much of their money in the stock market, then lie awake and worry about it. They continue to watch CNBC to see what the markets are doing. They continue to log into their accounts, hoping and praying that their accounts haven't gone down, and none of it is necessary.

"As Dr. Bernstein asks in his books, once you've won the game, why on earth would you keep playing?

"Warren Buffett had a perfect quote that relates to this."

It's insane to risk what you have for something you don't need.[6]

Jill found this idea fascinating.

"I can assure you that I'm not playing the game just for fun. When we've won, I want to know so we can stop."

"Aha!" Super Retirement Planner exclaimed. "You see, so many people don't actually know when they've won the game. That is something you will learn through our lessons.

---

6   Butler, David. "10 Lessons From Warren Buffett." *The Motley Fool*, The Motley Fool, 7 Jan. 2020, https://www.fool.com/investing/2020/01/07/10-lessons-from-warren-buffett.aspx.

"Hopefully, you can see why I wanted to take all of this time to review each of these timeless truths before getting to the retirement secret. Speaking of which, I think we may now be ready for it. Should we continue?"

Jack almost jumped out of his chair. "We're ready for the secret!"

"Okay, here we go!"

SUMMARY OF MAJOR POINTS

- The purpose of your money is most affected by the phase of your investing lifetime you currently reside in.
- The retirement secret applies to everyone differently, depending on their circumstances.
- Therefore, the first investing phase occurs when you're young AND saving for decades into the future, and the blinders strategy is likely the best approach for you.
- The last investing phase comes during retirement and, for most, means focusing on income and preservation, not growth.
- The most challenging stage of your investing life span is the middle investing phase, where you transition from accumulating to preserving and generating your retirement income.
- The specific moment in which your finances may be at greatest risk may very well be the date of your retirement.
- If saving and investing throughout your life is a "game" you're trying to win to be able to retire, once you've "won the game," why on earth would you continue playing?

Chapter 5

=====

YOUR RETIREMENT BLUEPRINT

"Finertia: paralysis by analysis brought on by trying to compre-hend contradicting and confusing financial information."

—GREGORY SALSBURY, *RETIREMENTOLOGY*

Super Retirement Planner began the explanation that Jack and Jill had been dying to hear.

"Let me summarize once more to ensure we're on the same page. We know that there is no such thing as a perfect investment. We know that your purpose should dictate how you handle your money, and finally, we know that your purpose is most affected by the phase of your investing lifetime that you're currently in."

"Absolutely. Believe me, we're on the same page," Jill said with confidence.

Super Retirement Planner nodded and continued. "Now, it would be logical to assume that there would be 'one way' to invest that was agreed upon by the so-called experts. But in fact, it's the exact opposite. If you interviewed one hundred financial professionals, you would probably get one hundred different recommendations.

"Now, there are different reasons for that. For example, I think it's fair to assume that some of it might be due to the advisor having a conflict of interest and 'pushing' their clients in one direction or another.

"But there is an underappreciated truth when it comes to hiring someone to help you with your finances."

> THERE IS NO SUCH THING AS AN UNBIASED
> FINANCIAL PROFESSIONAL.

"It is impossible," Super Retirement Planner added. "Because to provide you with any kind of guidance, the professional must have an opinion. Although bias is often used with a negative connotation, that's not how I mean it here. I simply mean that every financial professional favors one or more investment philosophies over others.

"As an example, let's say you meet an investment advisor who tells you they don't believe in managed mutual funds or picking stocks; they think everyone is best off in an index fund. Then you meet with another who believes that picking smart money managers is the key to successful investing. Both advisors have a bias based on their philosophy.

"I'll give you another quick example from stories clients have told me. Let's say you consider yourself a pretty conservative person, and you go talk to an investment advisor who believes that investors should have all their money in stocks and bonds. When you tell them you're conservative, they may respond by putting about half of your money into stocks and half into bonds. Then 2008 happens, and your 'conservative' portfolio loses 30 percent. Do you think there may have been a philosophical mismatch there?"

"I can't imagine how angry I would be if my conservative portfolio lost 30 percent!" Jack said.

"Yet it happened to thousands of people around the country in the early 2000s and again in 2008," Super Retirement Planner replied. "And once again, in early 2020, many people lost a lot more than they expected to. Imagine the ones who had just retired—imagine how *they* felt!"

Jill stared straight ahead and simply said, "Terrified."

"You're exactly right," Super Retirement Planner continued. "It is so important to make sure your financial professional has a philosophy that matches yours.

"But guess what? There is another problem here. Dr. Pfau describes it in his book *Safety-First Retirement Planning*.

> The financial services profession is divided between two camps: those focusing on investment solutions and those focusing on insurance solutions. Both sides have their adherents who see little use for the other side. But the most efficient retirement strategies require an integration of both investments and insurance.

"Dr. Pfau is so right, and yet I believe he understates this. What he is saying is clear."

> BECAUSE OF THEIR PHILOSOPHIES, THE VAST
> MAJORITY OF FINANCIAL PROFESSIONALS WILL
> NOT AND CANNOT PROVIDE THEIR CLIENTS
> WITH AN OPTIMAL INVESTMENT PLAN.

"Now, doesn't that sound crazy?" Super Retirement Planner asked.

Jack and Jill again nodded their approval.

"Our firm's bias is simply this: we believe that in order to try to find each person's optimal investment plan, the only logical way to do so is to consider all of the solutions that are available."

"Holy cow!" Jack exclaimed. "I feel like an idiot because that's what I assumed all financial people would do."

Jill put her hand on Jack's. "Don't feel that way, honey. I'm pretty sure that's what we all assumed."

Super Retirement Planner had seen this before.

"Please don't beat yourself up. It is simply the way things work in our industry. Keep in mind, the vast majority of those professionals truly believe they are doing the best thing. Now you know that their biases exist, and more importantly, you know you don't have to be limited by them!

"Let me cover one last topic that explains why I believe this secret is so valuable before we jump into the specifics. Regarding how to invest your money, author Dr. Bernstein writes:

In the real world of investing, you are faced with a seemingly limitless choice of assets which can be combined into a literally infinite number of portfolios.

"If you've ever done any research into trying to find the 'best' investments, I'm sure you know how true this is!"

Jill jabbed Jack in the side with her elbow.

"Yeah, I have to admit it," Jack said. "At one point, I thought I could figure out the perfect investment mix, but I found what I was looking at definitely felt limitless and infinite."

Super Retirement Planner nodded understandingly.

"Remember, the two of you were thrust into this job of managing your own retirement plan with no training. Don't be too hard on yourselves. It would be silly to have expected you to handle your money perfectly throughout your lifetime. This discussion isn't about the past. It's about the future.

"Okay, so we've already talked about how there are no perfect investments, which means we have to diversify."

> DON'T PUT ALL YOUR EGGS INTO ONE BASKET!

"I'm sure that isn't a news flash for you, but it's true. Most financially devastating situations occur because someone puts all their faith into one thing. Think of the worst investment decision you ever made and how much you lost. Now imagine if you had put every single dollar you owned into it!"

Jack put his head into his hands.

"Oh my goodness, I think she would have divorced me!"

"We can laugh about it now because it didn't happen," Super Retirement Planner said, "but financial stress is one of the biggest reasons marriages fail. Sadly, it happens all the time.

"So we don't want to put all your eggs into one basket. We also need to find investments that are *uncorrelated*. That is a fancy investment word that means finding things that don't act the same way, or in other words, act differently from each other. Let's use a really simple example: let's say you own a bunch of stock in Apple. Of course, Apple stock has done quite well over the years, but if you have all your eggs in that one basket, it can be a wild ride!

"How can you reduce that risk? Well, what if you sold half of your Apple stock and used that money to buy Samsung stock?"

Jill mustered the courage to speak first.

"I mean, it would have to reduce your risk at least a little since you now have two baskets instead of one. But it seems like a pretty similar basket, right?"

Super Retirement Planner leaned back with a big smile.

"Wow, Jill, that was the exact right answer! Yes, it helps a little, but Samsung is Apple's biggest cell phone competitor, so that is a very similar basket. Maybe to reduce risk, instead of Samsung, you could buy a more unrelated stock like Walmart.

"Or maybe you could invest in something that's not even a stock. We'll get to whatever that 'other' thing might be later.

"All right, let's move on to one final quote from Dr. Bernstein.

> The right asset mix becomes apparent only in retrospect; the optimal mix for the next twenty years is unlikely to look anything like the optimal mix for the past twenty years. How on God's green earth do you find the best future asset mix?

"Dr. Bernstein is getting at a couple of important points. First, of course, we can't predict the future. He's just making sure we don't forget! He makes a simple but powerful point."

DIVERSIFYING OUR MONEY CAN BE
DIFFICULT AND COMPLICATED.

"The power of the retirement secret is that it takes this enormous task and makes it easy to understand."

Super Retirement Planner took a deep breath.

"All right, are you ready to see it?"

Jack leaped up and said, "Yes!"

Super Retirement Planner laughed and presented this:

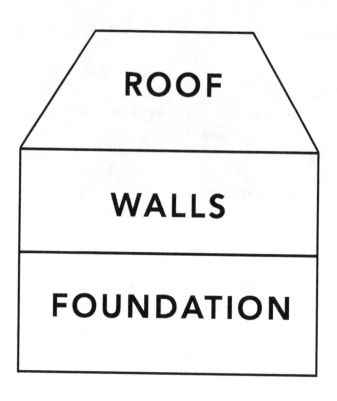

Jack looked it over and said, "Uh, okay. Is this it?"

Super Retirement Planner chuckled. "Don't worry, I know it doesn't look like much. Let me explain.

"Remember a few minutes ago when we were talking about there being literally millions of places you could put your savings and investments? How in the world can anyone make any decisions or keep track of all of that? This is the solution.

"Think of when a construction team is building a house. Although the entire process is very complex, at its most basic, you have a foundation at the bottom, walls along the sides, and a roof on top. We're going to use these three areas, but instead of building a home you're going to live in, this is how we're going to divvy up your nest egg.

"Like so many other people, you've expressed that you're unsure of how to invest your money. This will be like a blueprint for your nest egg. Not only does this give you clarity and direction of how to allocate your life savings, but it also gives you something to refer back to when making investment decisions in the future.

"Let's quickly go over the basics of the three levels: the level we call the Foundation is where accounts go that have some kind of underlying safety or guarantee. The Roof is where accounts go that fluctuate with the day-to-day swings of the market, and the Walls naturally is where accounts go that are in between the other two levels.

"By separating your options into these three levels, we can deal with the fact that there are no perfect investments. We can put the appropriate amount of money in the right areas based on what you're trying to accomplish. We can accommodate the fact that you are at an extremely sensitive time in your investing lives; we can set up your initial allocation and monitor it in a simple and understandable way; and finally, we can incorporate everything in the world of savings and investments instead of eliminating some of the possible solutions due to a certain philosophy.

"As we discussed before, the purpose of your money is to help you accomplish your goals, and for most planning for retirement, that means generating income to enjoy and never running out of money. To accomplish these goals, you need your nest egg to be protected from everything that puts you in danger."

Super Retirement Planner then expressed the dangers the way the seven retirement villains see them:

1. **Lady Longevity:** outliving your money
2. **The Invisible Enemy:** inflation-eating spending power
3. **Evil Uncle Sam:** excessive taxation
4. **Sarah Self-Pay:** out-of-pocket medical expenses
5. **Iceberg Ivan:** excessive investment expenses
6. **Systematic Sammy:** overdependence on the stock market in retirement
7. **Antiquated Andy:** outdated investing strategies

"Think of all the things our physical house protects us from. We can't know for certain what might threaten our home: flood, hurricane, tornado, fire, falling trees, and so on. If you knew in advance, you could design it more precisely. Since we don't know for certain, we build our house to protect ourselves as best we can from all of these risks. This is exactly what we do when we design your blueprint."

Super Retirement Planner paused before summarizing.

"All of this means that we can help you design how to divvy up your nest egg in a way that ultimately will give you the best chance at accomplishing your retirement dreams."

Super Retirement Planner let those final words settle in.

Jill responded first. "Wow, that sounds amazing."

"I agree," Jack added. "I'm a little fuzzy on what exactly goes into each of the three levels. Can you explain in a little more detail?"

"Oh, don't you worry, Jack," Super Retirement Planner said. "You're going to get into plenty of details! But not from me. You see, we've already gone too long today. What I think will be far more valuable is for you to meet three more people."

"Oh no, please tell me there aren't more retirement villains!" Jack interjected.

Super Retirement Planner smiled. "I promise no more villains. Now it's going to be time for you to meet the three Blueprint Mentors. Each of these three mentors will tell you all of the ins and outs of their particular level.

"Now, before you meet them, let me make sure you know a few important details.

"The three Blueprint Mentors are not villains, and they are not superheroes. They are extremely knowledgeable. They know everything about their particular level: the good, the bad, and the ugly, and they will share all of that with you.

"However, please keep in mind that they are biased. Although they know there is no such thing as a perfect investment, each of them lives on their particular level. Therefore, they *are* biased. Remember when I said you can't find unbiased financial information?"

Jack and Jill smiled and nodded.

Super Retirement Planner continued, "Talking with these three mentors is actually excellent practice for you. Just like you need to ask questions of financial professionals, you need to quiz these mentors as well. So anytime they tell you something great about their level, make sure to ask them about the downside.

"Any questions?" Super Retirement Planner asked.

Jack responded, "When do we meet them?"

Super Retirement Planner smiled and said, "If you knew ahead of time, that wouldn't be any fun."

Jack smiled, looked at Jill, and said, "Somehow, I knew that would be the answer."

SUMMARY OF MAJOR POINTS

- There is no such thing as an unbiased financial professional.
- Because of their philosophical biases, the vast majority of financial professionals will not and cannot provide their clients with an optimal investment plan.
- The only logical approach to seeking out your optimal investment plan is to consider all of the solutions that are available.
- Investing involves seemingly limitless options, which can be combined into a literally infinite number of allocations.
- First and foremost, don't put all your eggs into one basket!
- We know how important it is to diversify our money, but doing so can be difficult and complicated.
- The goal of the "retirement secret" is to take the enormous task of allocating your money and make it easy to understand.

Chapter 6

===

WALL STREET WILLIAM

Jack and Jill headed home. In the car, they chatted about the revelation of the retirement secret and how much they had learned.

Jack couldn't get the three Blueprint Mentors out of his mind as they stood in the kitchen, discussing what to have for dinner. He was itching to meet them.

"Which one do you think we'll meet first?"

Jill was searching the refrigerator for leftovers and popped her head up. "Gosh, the logical one would be the Foundation, right? That's where you would start when you're building something."

Jack chuckled. "Yeah, it would be pretty weird to start out with the Roof." Instantly, a huge puff of smoke filled the room!

Jack exclaimed, "Oh my goodness! This must be the first one already!"

When the smoke cleared, they saw a handsome man in his early forties. He was wearing a navy-blue suit that obviously cost thousands of dollars, a clean and crisp white dress shirt, and a bold, red power tie. He was carrying an expensive briefcase.

"Hello, I'm Wall Street William. It's a pleasure to meet you!"

"Hi, I'm Jack, and this is my wife, Jill. For a second there, I thought you were that guy from the movie *Wall Street*."

"Oh yeah, Michael Douglas!" Jill interjected.

"Yes, indeed. I get that quite often!"

He walked over to the kitchen table, opened his briefcase, and sat down with a confident smile on his face.

"Shall we get down to business?"

Jack and Jill scrambled to grab their notepads. Wall Street William could be quite intimidating! With their pens in hand, they quickly sat down and nodded.

"Super Retirement Planner has given me a very clear task," Wall Street William began. "My job is to make sure you understand what the Roof is, the purpose of its investments typically, the pros and cons of Roof investing, and examples of Roof investments. We have a lot to cover, so let's get started.

"First, are you wondering why you're starting with me?"

Jack and Jill nodded again.

"It's actually for a simple reason: as I'm sure Super Retirement Planner has discussed, the American retirement system has shifted to a focus on the 401(k). So now, millions of Americans are relying on these plans to provide them with a comfortable retirement. The vast majority of your investment options in your 401(k) are Roof investments, so Super Retirement Planner always likes everyone to start with me."

WHAT ARE ROOF INVESTMENTS?

"Roof investments can be affected by the day-to-day and sometimes minute-to-minute swings of the news, stock market, and economy," Wall Street William explained. "You can think quickly about some places you can put your money that do and don't fit into that description. The mutual funds in your 401(k) can change in value every day, so they fit into the Roof, but if the stock market crashes, that doesn't affect the money you have in your savings account. Does that quick comparison make sense?"

"Definitely. I think our savings account would be in the Foundation, right?" Jill added.

William waved his hand dismissively. "I only concern myself with the Roof. Now, before digging into details, let me quickly share a list of investments that we would consider fitting into the Roof."

He then listed example of Roof investments:

- Stocks
- Mutual funds
- Bonds (but not US Savings Bonds)
- Variable annuity account values

WHY INVEST IN THE ROOF?

"As Super Retirement Planner always says, what you're trying to accomplish should determine where you put your money. So what would you be trying to accomplish by investing in the Roof? Hopefully, the first one is obvious."

THE POTENTIAL FOR GROWTH

"Many Roof investments offer the potential for great upside. This potential has historically been tied to the stock market, but there are other options that we'll discuss later. Let's stop for a second and dig into this point. The reason investors want growth isn't really for the growth itself. Sure, it's great to see your values go up, but what good does that actually do you? For someone in retirement, there are two reasons this can be really important: longevity and inflation—"

"Lady Longevity and the Invisible Enemy!" Jill interjected.

William didn't like being interrupted, but Jill was right.

"Correct. The reason so many retirees still invest seeking growth is because they don't know how long their retirement will be, and they don't know how much anything is going to cost in the future. For these reasons, you can't just leave your money in a checking account or buried under your mattress.

"Now, let me also mention that there are two additional reasons so many people put money into the Roof."

ACCESSIBILITY AND FLEXIBILITY

"Many Roof options allow you to get in and out of them on a quarterly, daily, or even minute-by-minute basis. This access could be tremendously valuable if you have unexpected needs and must quickly access a portion of your nest egg.

"Easy access is beneficial not only in case of an emergency. It also provides valuable flexibility in case there is a need or desire to adjust the allocation of your nest egg. For example, there could be shifts in the economic landscape, changes to specific investment solutions, or transitions in your life or your goals. Soon you'll learn about options in the Foundation and Walls that may have lots of great characteristics, but they may require you to tie up your money for months or even years. Although that's fine for some of your money, you obviously want to have some flexibility built into your overall plan, and the Roof can provide that."

William finally stopped and took a breath. He had been talking so confidently and without hesitation that Jack and Jill weren't sure if he was even interested in letting them ask questions. Jill mustered up her courage.

"So people invest in the Roof for the potential for growth, accessibility, and flexibility," she said. "That makes sense."

"Excellent!" William did *not* have time for slowpokes! "Let's dig into my favorite part: the pros of the Roof! When it comes to long-term averages, it's tough to beat the stock market. Check out this chart that goes way back to 1802 from Jeremy Siegel, Professor of Finance at the Wharton School of the University of Pennsylvania and author of the book *Stocks for the Long Haul*."

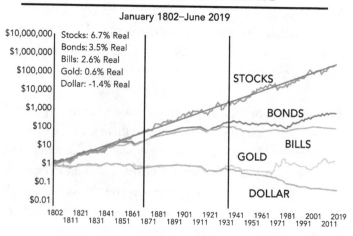

Total Real Return Indexes

January 1802–June 2019

Stocks: 6.7% Real
Bonds: 3.5% Real
Bills: 2.6% Real
Gold: 0.6% Real
Dollar: -1.4% Real

Source: Siegel, Jeremy. Stocks for the Long Run (2014). With updates to 2019.

"The remarkable thing about this chart is not only how much better the stock performance is than the other investments, but also how steady they are. As you can see, the chart shows almost a straight line!

"One quick point to make is the term *real* in the chart. That just means that is the average rate of return after inflation. For example, if stocks earned 9.7 percent and inflation was 3 percent that year, then we would say the real rate of return was 6.7 percent.

"Another great thing about the Roof is the idea of dollar-cost averaging. As Investopedia.com explains, 'Dollar-cost averaging is a strategy that allows an investor to buy the same dollar amount of an investment on regular intervals. The purchases occur regardless of the asset's price. A perfect example of dollar-cost averaging is its use in 401(k) plans. An employee can select a predetermined amount of their salary that they wish to invest in a menu of mutual or index funds.'

"I know that Super Retirement Planner will often use this approach with his clients who are still working. The beauty of dollar-cost averaging is that it helps you if the stock market were to drop. You see, if the stock market goes down, your 401(k) contribution is still buying shares. Since the share price has gone down, you will automatically buy more shares. Guess what you just did? You 'bought low'!"

William paused here, hoping Jack and Jill were impressed.

Jack thought about this new information. "Okay, that makes sense. I don't know if I would be really excited about that because if the market is down, that still means I lost money."

William again waved his hand at Jack.

"Well, sure, you lost money, but only temporarily. Remember the chart we just looked at? Eventually, that investment will probably go back up, right?"

"Hopefully!" Jill replied with a smile.

William refused to let Jill slow him down. "All right, so as you can see, the Roof can have lots of benefits! Any questions?"

Jack and Jill looked at each other.

"Oh yeah, Super Retirement Planner told us that William would be really excited about the Roof!" Jill said. "He told us the good, but we need to ask him about the bad and the ugly. All right, William, what's the downside?"

"Aw, rats!" William shouted as he slammed his fist on the kitchen table. "This is the part I do not enjoy. All right, let's do it."

HOW ROOF INVESTMENTS CAN HURT YOU

"First, we will start with what is probably an obvious downside: since investments in the Roof can change at any moment, that means that they can drop in value.

"Whenever I share the chart above, Super Retirement Planner always wants me to also share this chart from 2000–09."[7]

---

7   "The Number 1 Reason To Be A Dividend Growth Investor (And It's Not What You Were Expecting)." *SeekingAlpha*, https://seekingalpha.com/article/4163977-number-1-reason-dividend-growth-investor-expecting.

S&P 5000

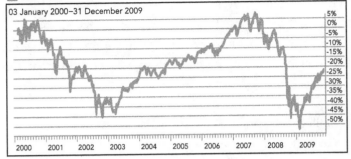

03 January 2000–31 December 2009

"Here's another one Super Retirement Planner makes me show. This one is just from late 2007 through early 2009."[8]

$SPX S&P 500 Large Cap Index INDX

9-Mar-2009 **Op** 680.76 **Hi** 695.27 **Cl** 676.53 **Vol** 5.3B **Chg** -6.85 (1.00%)

$SPX (Daily) 676.53 (9 Mar)

2007–2009

Jack's face curled up in disgust.

"Oh my goodness, I can't even see those charts without my chest tightening up," he said. "I remember those days and how scared I was. You could never tell if the market was going to go back up or if it was going to keep going down!"

---

8   "Big Rallies Are Common In Bear Markets." *SeekingAlpha*, https://seekingalpha.com/article/3896576-big-rallies-common-bear-markets.

William rolled his eyes. "Yeah, well, I wasn't worried, and it turned out fine, right? I do have to mention that although, in these cases, the stock market recovered within years, a quick recovery is certainly not guaranteed. Let me read from *The Little Book of Safe Money*.

> Millions of investors have come to believe that if you just hold on to stocks long enough, they become risk-free. US stocks lost 89 percent of their value between 1929 and 1932. In Japan at the end of 1989, the leading Nikkei 225 stock index was at 38,915.87; two decades later, it languishes below 10,000, a nearly 75 percent loss.

"The technical term of this risk of values dropping is called volatility risk. This just means your money in the Roof is exposed to the risk of volatile pricing."

Jack interrupted, "Thanks, Captain Obvious!" He was still in a bad mood, thinking about his losses in 2008.

William gave Jack a quick glare. "Anyway, Super Retirement Planner always points out that this risk affects how you allocate your money in a couple of ways."

> You should NEVER depend on the Roof to create your retirement income.

"Hopefully, the reason for this is obvious. Although the long-term averages have been great, in the short term, you just can't know what the markets will bring, and you don't want to base the success of your retirement on hope."

"William," Jill was scribbling on her notepad, "that was amazing.

I seriously think what you just said might be the summary of my whole retirement plan: you don't want to base the success of your retirement on hope."

"You're welcome, I guess." William wasn't used to getting compliments and wasn't sure how to respond. "You've met Systematic Sammy. That is what we're talking about here. If you don't count on the Roof to generate your retirement income, then you don't have to worry about a stock market crash wiping out your retirement income."

"Right." Jill was becoming much more comfortable around William and interrupted without fear for the first time. "So I have a question, then. Once we retire, if our primary goal is to generate income, should we avoid the Roof completely?"

William rubbed his chin. "That's a great question. I talk with Super Retirement Planner all the time. Although he has said some people do choose to avoid the Roof, most retirees still keep some money here.

"The reason is simple: most people don't have a singular goal in retirement to create the highest income possible. In addition to creating a high income, most people would also like to try to have some growth and to also have some flexibility and accessibility."

"Ah, yes!" Jill was nodding, smiling, and making notes. "Of course, it all comes back to what we want our money to help us accomplish. I have to keep in mind the timeless principles!"

William smiled. He didn't often feel empathy for anyone else, yet for some reason, he did at this moment. "Oh, there is definitely a lot to remember," he added.

"Well, thank you," Jill said with a smile. "I sincerely appreciate that. Now let's keep this moving!"

"Right!" William placed both of his hands onto the table. "Where was I? Oh, yes! Volatility risk: in addition to risking your retirement income, it's important to keep in mind that this can affect your flexibility and accessibility. This is because you may need to access that money at the same time when the value is down. Even though you *can* access your money, you may not *want* to. Does that make sense?"

"Yep." Jack was sure he understood. "If I needed to get at some of my money at the end of 2008, I had about half of what I was hoping would be there."

William nodded at the accuracy of his statement while ignoring the comment about losing money. "Great. Now I'll share the next 'string attached' to Roof investments. I will admit that this is one I really hate sharing."

Jack and Jill both moved to the edge of their seats.

"That is a great lead-in. You have our undivided attention!" Jill said.

ARE YOUR INVESTMENTS' AVERAGE RETURNS REAL?

"Remember the chart where I showed you the long-term returns of the stock market? Well, many experts believe that those returns aren't really true and that people from Wall Street should never show them. Let's start with this quote about the 'big lie' from Patrick Kelly in *Stress-Free Retirement*.

Sometimes a lie is told so incredibly well that even those perpetrating it believe it as truth. Such is the case with stock market averages. Here's the bitter truth. The "average" returns reported by financial companies are not reality.

"You see, rate of return is actually made up of two types of return: average return and actual, or annualize, return. The only difference is when you experience a loss. Imagine a hypothetical account that makes 50 percent in the first year and then loses 50 percent in the next year. Over those two years, what is the average return?"

Jack and Jill hesitated before Jack said, "I think it's 0 percent."

"That's right," William confirmed. "But now let's do the math in dollars. If you invested $100,000 and made 50 percent, your account would be worth $150,000. But now, you lose 50 percent, and your account would be worth only $75,000, or a 25 percent loss. Why is this? **Anytime you have one year of losses, your average return will not equal your actual return.**

"This makes a bigger difference over time. From 1900 through the end of 2019, the average return of the Dow Jones was 7.4 percent per year. However, the actual or annualized return was only 5.2 percent per year. That means that the actual returns of investors over that time frame would be almost a third less than what was expected!"[9]

"Wait, wait, wait!" Jack stopped William. He was angry. "Do you mean to tell me that my investments can tell me I've made an

9   https://www.crestmontresearch.com/docs/Stock-Average.pdf.

average of 7.4 percent a year, but in reality, I've actually made only 5.2 percent?"

William nodded. Jack was completely flustered. "That's insane!"

William had seen people get angry before. "I know it sounds crazy, but that is how the math works when you add in negative returns. I would summarize with this: just remember that annualized returns are always less than average returns, and unfortunately, you pay your bills with annualized returns. **And WE Make It Worse!**

"Now let me share two specific examples. The first is from Keith Stanovich's book *What Intelligence Tests Miss: The Psychology of Rational Thought*:

> Consider for a moment a very volatile period of the stock market, from the beginning of 1998 to the end of 2001. During that period, the Firsthand Technology Value mutual fund did very well. Its average gain for this period was 16 percent per year. Yet the average investor who invested in this fund lost 31.6 percent of his or her money over this same four-year period.

"Now, that is an extreme example! This one may be even more shocking: one of the more startling examples is a study conducted by Fidelity on the performance of its flagship Magellan mutual fund. The fund was run by investment legend Peter Lynch, who delivered an astonishing 29 percent average annual return between 1977 and 1990, but Fidelity found the average Magellan investor actually *lost* money."[10]

---

10 Tony Robbins, *Money: Master the Game* (New York, NY: Simon and Schuster, 2019).

William paused when he saw Jack and Jill's jaws dropping.

"Yes, that means that one of the most successful mutual funds in the history of investing had a lot of investors lose money," he added.

Jack was a basket of emotions. He was angry that he felt he had been lied to. He was embarrassed because he felt he had been sold a bill of goods, and he had fallen for it. He was confused and wondering why anyone would invest in the stock market.

"This is ridiculous!" he said. "Those big-shot money managers are ripping everyone off!"

William realized he had pushed Jack a little too far.

"Hang on, Jack. Yes, the 'average returns' thrown around by Wall Street can be really misleading, but please keep in mind these results weren't only because of the so-called volatility gremlins. These investors also struggled because of how difficult it is for us to deal with investments that go up and down in value frequently. It has been proven time and again that most investors just can't handle a bumpy ride.

"We often see the markets going up, then jump in late in the game. Then, when the markets fall, we panic because we see our account balances going down. Over and over again, this leads investors to buy high and sell low—literally the exact opposite of what we're supposed to do. Super Retirement Planner often tells me that seeing this repeatedly during his career makes him very cautious with stock market investments.

"In fact, one of the most revered names in investment history,

Benjamin Graham, said, *'The investor's chief problem—and even his worst enemy—is likely to be himself.'*[11]

Jack was still upset. "Okay, so maybe the stock market isn't where we want to put our money in retirement. What other options are there?"

ROOF OPTIONS OTHER THAN THE STOCK MARKET

"That's a great question," William responded. "Let's quickly go over another option that is commonly used in retirees' portfolios: bonds. Although bonds and bond funds can be useful for investors, there are numerous things to consider. First, let me read you these quotes from two of the most successful investors of all time. First, David Swensen, Investment Officer of the Yale endowment since 1985, in his acclaimed book *Pioneering Portfolio Management*:

'Unfortunately for investors, corporate bonds contain a variety of unattractive characteristics, including credit risk, illiquidity, and callability.'"

William continued, "Even though I love David Swensen, he does write in a very technical manner. I would summarize his feelings that bond investors need to be careful. For something a little easier to understand, this is what Warren Buffett has said, *'Bonds should come with a warning label.'*

"So why would these two say things like this? I would summarize it like this: a lot of financial professionals like to think that bonds are 'safe' or 'risk-free.' But bonds clearly do not fit into the

---

11   https://quotefancy.com/quote/1559500/Benjamin-Graham-The-investor-s-chief-problem-and-even-his-worst-enemy-is-likely-to-be.

Foundation of the house. They fit into the Roof. This is simply because their value can change at any time. Yes, the value can go up, but the value can also go down.

Wall Street William then went on to read a few points from *The Little Book of Safe Money*:

- *Short-term bond funds, often sold as being "safe as cash," are no such thing. In 2008, the Schwab YieldPlus short-term bond fund lost 35.4 percent.*
- *Consider the Oppenheimer Core Bond fund, which lost 36 percent in 2008. According to its own documents, the fund was intended to provide "income," "protection of principle," and "preservation of capital" by investing in intermediate-term bonds."*

"Hopefully, you can see why it can be very dangerous to throw around terms like *moderate* or *moderately conservative* portfolios," William said. "A lot of well-meaning financial professionals will recommend portfolios that may be around half stocks and half bonds, and sometimes those portfolios will do really well, but sometimes they will do very poorly."

Jack and Jill looked at each other. They looked tired. Hearing so many examples of what could go wrong was exhausting.

Finally, Jack looked back at William.

"I've got to be honest," he said. "At this point, I'm not sure I even want a single dollar of our nest egg in the Roof."

William smiled. "Believe it or not, I completely understand, but there are four strategies that Super Retirement Planner does like to use in the Roof. If he thinks they're worth considering, then we should review them. Super Retirement Planner and his team are the ones to talk to in detail, but I can give you a quick explanation."

COMMON PREFERRED ROOF STRATEGIES
1. DIVERSIFIED, LOW-COST STOCK MARKET INVESTING

"This is the first choice Super Retirement Planner considers. Boy, that sounds exciting, doesn't it?" William laughed at his own joke.

Jack and Jill looked at each other and snickered before William continued talking.

"Diversified, low-cost investing simply follows the philosophy that you cannot predict or 'beat' the markets. Therefore, the goal is to keep costs as low as absolutely possible. The advantage of this style of investing is that you will essentially capture all of the upside of the markets when they are increasing.

"Of course, that clearly means that you will capture all of the losses when the markets drop!

"This strategy can only work if you as the investor are committed to holding on to the investments through a downturn, and for this reason, it does not usually make up a huge portion of your investments because of the risk of loss it leaves you open to."

"Heck, yeah," Jack sighed. "Back in 2008, I reached a point when I couldn't bear to even open my 401(k) statements when they came in the mail!"

"Exactly," William agreed. "Now, you can reduce the risk at least a little with some simple diversification." He then explained that meant investing in stock funds such as:

- Large US companies
- Small or medium-sized US companies
- Developed international companies
- Emerging markets international companies

"Although many markets move up and down similarly, holding a mixture at least provides a small amount of diversity."

William could see that Jack and Jill were following right along with him, so he carried on.

2. TACTICAL INVESTING

"In a nutshell, this is a strategy that gives the portfolio manager complete control to shift between various types of investments. Now, keep in mind, this does *not* mean that we're expecting the manager to be able to predict the markets! Rather, this allows the manager to shift based on pricing. For example, if the manager sees that US markets are overpriced and that bond markets are underpriced, they may decide to shift some of the funds at that time.

"The purpose of tactical investing is not seeking higher returns. Instead, the primary goal of tactical investing is to reduce the risk of loss. Theoretically, when stock markets are overpriced, like in 2000 and 2008, this model would allow the manager to have already shifted a portion of the portfolio into safer investments before the stock markets began dropping.

"The downside of this type of investing is that it will definitely have lower returns than the stock market when markets are booming. An investor in this type of portfolio has to be willing to 'miss out' if the markets go way up."

Jack jumped in. "Wait, so you're telling me that I can't have *all* the upside with *no* downside? No fair!"

He then let out a hearty laugh.

William shook his head and let a smirk slip.

"Yes, you are correct. No matter how many times someone might imply there is a way to do that, you know very well that is impossible since there are no perfect investments!

"Now, the other downside compared to low-cost investing is that since it is managed, there will be management fees. The bottom line here is to always consider the potential return for how much risk you're taking as well as the fees you're paying."

3. ENDOWMENT PORTFOLIO APPROACH[12]

"Since I know you've met all of the retirement villains, I'm sure you remember Antiquated Andy and how he taught you about

---

12   There are material differences between the terms under which endowments and individuals can invest in alternative investments. These differences include, but are not limited to, commissions and fees, conflicts of interest, access to investment opportunities, size, investment time horizons, and the ability to tolerate illiquidity. There is no standard or exact definition of the endowment model. Portfolio design, specific investments, and ultimately, performance vary considerably among endowments and investors. Kalos does not claim that any investor will achieve the same result as any endowment, institution, or other investor. Kalos's Investment Adviser Representatives have a conflict of interest when they recommend securities where they earn a commission as Registered Representatives of Kalos Capital. We address this conflict by disclosing the fees and commissions related to the investments recommended to our clients. Also, Kalos representatives do not earn both advisory fees and brokerage commissions on the same assets.

the idea of how endowments invest their money by using all kinds of different investment options beyond stocks and bonds," William said.

Jack and Jill nodded.

"Good," William continued. "This strategy involves finding a money manager who will use the investment and asset allocation strategies similar to how the largest endowments in the world use them. Think of this as a 'one-stop shop' of endowment investing.

"Super Retirement Planner believes the biggest benefit of this type of strategy is the ability to seek growth without having to be exclusively or even primarily invested in the stock market. Hopefully, if a big stock market drop occurs, this type of fund will be able to preserve much more principal than a typical stock portfolio.

"On the downside, an endowment portfolio approach will most likely have at least somewhat limited access to your funds. One example would be a portfolio that gives you access to withdrawals but only once every ninety days. Even though ninety days isn't a very long time, it is much less accessible than many 'Roof' options, which provide daily or even minute-by-minute access.

"Just like tactical strategies, these are also managed, which means it will have portfolio fees as well. Once again, it's not that all fees are bad. The particular strategy simply must be able to warrant the cost of the fees."

4. PRIVATE EQUITY

"This may sound like an odd name," Wall Street William said. "But it's actually quite simple: the regular stock market is sometimes referred to as the 'equities' market. In the world of investing, equity simply refers to ownership. If you own a share of Apple stock, that means you are a part owner of the company. A very tiny part owner but a part owner nonetheless!

"Private equity simply means investing in ownership of companies that have not gone public. Now, if you're like me, when you think of large companies, you assume that they're public, but in fact, many companies choose to never go public.

"Here's a quick list of some of the bigger private companies that you may be familiar with," he added and then supplied the names.

- Aldi Supermarkets
- State Farm Insurance
- IKEA
- Publix
- Mars Candies
- Chick-Fil-A"[13]

"Wow," Jill interjected. "Those are some great companies, and they're so big that I would have assumed they were public."

"Yes, in fact, Aldi's sales in 2017 were more than $13 billion!" William responded.[14] "What are the specific reasons Super

---

13   Wikipedia, "List of Largest Private Nongovernmental Companies by Revenue." https://wikipedia.org/wiki/List_of_largest_private_non-governmental_companies_by_revenue.

14   Reagan, Courtney. "Grocer Aldi Targets Nearby Rivals in Its Bid to Boost Its US Footprint." *CNBC*, CNBC, 9 Aug. 2018, https://www.cnbc.com/2018/08/08/grocer-aldi-targets-nearby-rivals-in-bid-to-its-boost-its-us-footprint.html.

Retirement Planner believes considering private equity is a good idea? I would summarize it in three points:

"The first reason to consider private equity is simply a continuation of what you've already been learning: it is yet another asset class and therefore provides additional diversification. Although there are similarities, we would expect public and private stocks to react somewhat differently.

"The second reason is performance. Even though it is more challenging to track private equity returns, the index often compares favorably against the US stock market. Through September 30, 2018, the S&P 500 return over the previous twenty-five years was 9.81 percent per year."[15]

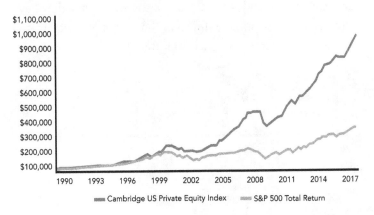

Cambridge US Private Equity Index   S&P 500 Total Return

Jack stopped William in his tracks. "Yeah, but that is average return and not annualized, right?"

William was impressed.

"Yes, you're right. An investor in the S&P 500 would not have

15   www.pomonainvestmentfund.com.

earned 9.81 percent per year. Because of the significant ups and downs, they would have earned much less. Now, during the same twenty-five years, the Cambridge Associates LLC Private Equity Index had an average of 13.42 percent per year.

"Now, one thing I have to make clear is that there is, of course, no proof that these types of returns will continue into the future, but they certainly show that this is a type of investment with promise," William said.

"The third and final reason to consider private equity is possibly the most important. Although the Roof is focused on long-term growth, ultimately for many investors, the goal is to minimize losses whenever possible. Even though private equity investments can and certainly have sustained losses, they have historically performed better than the public markets during the most difficult times. Check out this chart."[16]

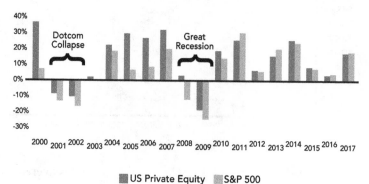

"Look very closely at 2001–02 and again at 2008–09. You'll notice that private equity lost money in three of those four years, but those losses were clearly less than what the public markets suffered."

16 Cambridge Associates US, Private Equity Index and Selected Benchmark Statistics (data as of 6/30/17).

Jack and Jill were impressed.

"Yes, we would love to always avoid losing, but we also understand that the Roof is about trying to get long-term growth, so it's not going to just go straight up," Jack responded. "Super Retirement Planner started us off by showing us that there are no perfect investments. So if private equity has strong long-term performance and has done well during bad times, what's the catch?"

William nodded and smiled.

"I have to admit, you have both impressed me with what quick learners you are! Yes, private equity has compelling features, but you're right; it's far from perfect. First, obviously, it's not perfect because you can see in the chart that it sometimes loses money.

"Second, these investments are managed, so they will have management fees associated with them.

"Third, access to these investments can be more limited than others. The account minimums are often higher than other investments. Currently, investors need to be able to allocate at least $50,000 or $100,000 to these types of strategies. Also, some portfolios may require that you meet an overall minimum net worth.

"Fourth and finally, since the money is invested into private companies, these investments are generally less accessible than investments in public markets. So it's important for investors and their planners to ensure they have accessible funds elsewhere when doing their planning."

William paused. Sometimes when he was finished with everything he knew he should cover, he could see exhaustion written across his students' faces. Sometimes overwhelm. Sometimes it was more of a "deer in the headlights" expression.

But with Jack and Jill, they looked comfortable and confident. They had followed William throughout the lesson and had taken good notes.

"I believe that is everything I have to cover. Do you have any questions?" he asked them.

Jack and Jill looked at each other.

"No, I don't think so," Jill replied. "This has been quite enlightening. William, it was a pleasure doing business with you."

Jack and Jill stood up, so William did as well. He grabbed his briefcase, and they all shook hands. As soon as his hand let go of Jill's, a cloud of smoke appeared.

Just like that, William was gone.

Jack chuckled. "That was sudden!"

Jill smiled. "It was. Okay, that was a ton of information. Let's make a list of the biggest things we took away from William."

Jack smiled back. "Honey, you have the best ideas."

SUMMARY OF MAJOR POINTS

- Roof investments can be defined as those that can be affected by the moment-to-moment swings of the news, stock market, and economy.

- The biggest reasons to invest in the Roof are for potential long-term growth as well as flexibility and accessibility.
- Another benefit of the Roof is for those still saving and investing before retirement. Dollar-cost averaging by investing systematically into an account like a 401(k) can help you "buy low" in cases where the stock market drops.
- Because of the potential to suffer significant losses, Roof investments should NOT be depended on for retirement income.
- Average returns marketed by Wall Street firms are not "real" returns. Roof investors must understand the difference between average returns and annualized returns.
- Because of our natural human desire to avoid loss, the psychology of Roof investing is extremely challenging for most. Therefore, all Roof investors must remember Benjamin Graham's famous quote: "The investor's chief problem, and even his worst enemy, is likely to be himself."
- Super Retirement Planner's most commonly used Roof options include:
    ◦ Diversified, low-cost stock market investing
    ◦ Tactical investing with the goal of minimizing losses
    ◦ Endowment portfolio approach
    ◦ Private equity

Chapter 7

===

SAFE SUSAN

"Beware the investment activity that produces applause; the great moves are usually greeted by yawns."

—WARREN BUFFETT

"In most cases, the ultimate object of a successful investment strategy is to minimize your chances of dying poor—to obtain portfolio returns that will allow you to sleep at night. In other words, to be...boring."

—WILLIAM BERNSTEIN, *THE FOUR PILLARS OF INVESTING*

Jack and Jill woke up and started their usual Saturday routine. Jack made sure the coffee was started and went out to pick up the morning paper. Jill took their collie, Lassie, out and made sure that she was fed.

They all met on the porch: Jack, Jill, Lassie, the paper, and two cups of coffee. It was a beautiful morning—a little crisp chill in the air, yet sunny enough to know that it would get warmer soon. It was perfect.

Jill took a sip of coffee and looked over at Jack. "How did you sleep?"

Rather than answer immediately, Jack pondered the question first. "So-so."

Jill could tell he was thinking about something. "Why do you think that is?"

Jack looked over at Jill and smiled. They had now been married for thirty-seven years, and she had been a counselor for much of that time. He had gotten used to her probing questions, and now he even knew to expect them.

"That's a great question, Counselor," he quipped as he winked at her. "I am trying to decide if I am sure why I didn't sleep perfectly. Maybe it's because I am excited about everything we're learning right now. Or maybe it's because I'm a little scared of learning about how difficult it is to get all this financial stuff right. Or maybe it's because it's just overwhelming." He paused and took a sip of coffee. "How about you?"

"Ditto."

They shared a big laugh. Jack knew Jill was joking and had more to say, and Jill knew that Jack knew.

"I have the same fears, but I am trusting the process," Jill continued. "I can see that we're getting answers, and I'm confident we'll have a plan soon. That's the most important thing to me. When I don't know what we're doing or what to expect, that's when I'm scared and when I lie awake worrying at night."

This bothered Jack.

"Gosh, honey, I hope what we've been doing up until now wasn't causing you to worry. I was trying my best to make sure we would be ready."

Jill smiled at Jack. "Thank you, dear. I'm not mad. It's just that I think it's impossible for most people to figure all this out on their own, and we didn't really even know that. So it's nothing that you did. It's just that we weren't prepared, but it's exciting to think that we will be soon. I just want our retirement to be safe!"

The exact moment the word *safe* left her lips, a huge puff of smoke filled the porch. Lassie jumped up and began barking feverishly. Jill grabbed her and calmed her down.

"Yes! Here we go!" Jack exclaimed.

Once the smoke settled, they saw a woman wearing a conservative blue dress and a white pearl necklace. She had short hair and a confident look. She appeared to be in her mid- to late sixties.

"Hello, my name is Safe Susan, and I'm your next Blueprint Mentor."

"Hi, Susan, we're very excited to meet you," Jill replied. "I have to say, you bear a striking resemblance to Margaret Thatcher!"

Jack was a history buff and got excited by the comparison. "Ah, yes, the first woman to be Prime Minister of the UK, not to mention the nickname of the Iron Lady!"

Susan showed a knowing smile.

"I get that a lot," she said. "Now, I'm a very busy person, so do you mind if we get started right away?"

Jill had gathered their pads of paper and pens. "Yes, we're definitely ready! I believe you appeared when I said the word *safe*, is that right?"

"That's correct," Susan responded. "I trust you've met my associate Wall Street William?"

"Oh, yes," Jack said. "We learned a lot. He's quite a character."

Susan smiled again. "Indeed, he is. I believe that you will find me more of an educator and less of a used-car salesman. Having said that, we have a tremendous amount to cover, so let's get started."

She perched herself on a chair and began.

"First, just like most people are puzzled by starting with the Roof, they're often confused as to why we would now move down to the Foundation. It's quite simple really: you started in the Roof because so many people are forced to invest there inside of 401(k) plans and other retirement accounts. We move on to the foundation because anyone saving for retirement has had at least some experience with safe accounts such as checking and savings accounts and CDs."

Within just a minute or two, Jack and Jill were already pretty sure they knew what to expect with Safe Susan: she was a confident, intelligent, no-nonsense straight shooter.

Both enjoyed the change of pace from Wall Street William and were excited to learn from her.

"This leads right into the definition of a Foundation account," Susan continued. "It's quite simple; a Foundation account provides a guarantee of your principal and/or of a lifetime income guarantee. Some of these options may only guarantee your principal. Some may only guarantee your income, and some may guarantee both, but those are details for later. Let me pause and make sure you're both with me so far."

She raised an eyebrow to signify that she was asking a question.

"Yes, absolutely," Jill replied despite feeling intimidated.

"Very good," Susan responded. She took her work very seriously and enjoyed it far more when her students were focused and followed along. So far, so good.

"Now let's discuss why we invest money in the Foundation. As I'm sure you remember, your purpose drives what you do with your money. However, the Foundation is unique in that we have a number of different reasons why someone might place a portion of their hard-earned money into the Foundation.

"These are the primary reasons someone places money into their Foundation," she said, then listed:

- Emergency reserve
- Safety of principal
- Lifetime guaranteed income

"So let's study these one by one along with examples of the types of accounts that are commonly used."

EMERGENCY RESERVE

"The first reason people allocate to the Foundation is to create an emergency reserve. This is money that needs to be easily accessible and to be protected from losing value. Although this is a basic concept that I'm sure you've heard before, many people wonder how much is the right amount for their emergency reserve. The financial textbook answer is typically to hold six months of living expenses here.

"Even though this is a good starting point, Super Retirement

Planner always likes me to point out that this can and should be customized to your own preferences. He likes to say, you should never have so little here that you become anxious, and since interest rates are so low, you should not hold more here than necessary.

"So what types of accounts make sense here? Your solution simply needs to provide you quick access and safety. A five-year certificate of deposit may be safe, but you can't access it without penalties, and a stock mutual fund will typically allow you to sell your shares whenever you want, but your money definitely isn't safe, so it shouldn't be used as an emergency fund.

"Most people put most or all their emergency reserve into their local or online bank checking, savings, or money market accounts. As long as they are FDIC insured, you should have peace of mind, as even in and around 2008, when hundreds of banks failed, most savers were fully protected.[17]

"Also, these types of accounts provide complete access and flexibility. Generally, this means you can withdraw your money either immediately or within a day or two.

"The downside to bank accounts is simple: low interest rates. Interest rates have been historically low for all types of bank accounts for over a decade, and as of right now, it appears that won't be changing anytime soon."[18]

---

17 https://en.wikipedia.org/wiki/
List_of_bank_failures_in_the_United_States_(2008%E2%80%93present).

18 "Federal Funds Rate - 62 Year Historical Chart." *MacroTrends*, https://www.macrotrends.
net/2015/fed-funds-rate-historical-chart.

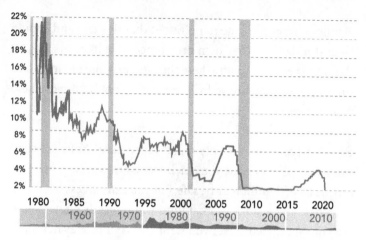

Jack snorted. "I think last month our bank accounts made 11 cents. As bad as that is, they have the audacity to call it a 'high-yield account'! How insulting is that?"

Jill patted Jack's arm. She knew this was a sensitive subject to Jack and that he liked to complain about it every chance he got.

Susan paused. Although she understood Jack's frustration, she knew complaining didn't solve anything.

"Anyway, bank accounts are perfect for your emergency reserve. Because of the low returns, they are generally not appropriate for the rest of your financial goals. I think we've covered this in enough detail, and I suggest we move on before your husband gets more upset."

Jill could see Susan giving her a knowing look. She smiled and nodded for Susan to continue.

SAFETY OF PRINCIPAL

"The second reason people place a portion of their nest egg into the Foundation is to provide safety of principal in addition to the emergency reserve. This relates directly to an idea I'm sure Super Retirement Planner has already covered with you: which phase of your investing lifetime you are in. For someone saving for retirement decades into the future, safety of principal is nice, but what they really need is to grow their money.

"However, when you are in the final phase of investing, you are retired and no longer working. You cannot expose all your life savings to the whims of the stock market, economy, and financial news. Therefore, you probably need to allocate a portion of your nest egg to the Foundation to protect it.

"Now, let's use a simple example of someone investing for retirement who has all of their portfolio in the stock market. We can say that they have the opportunity for excellent growth, but they are taking a lot of risk. There are actually two ways to reduce their risk:

1. **Avoid** the risk, or
2. Attempt to **manage** the risk

"Although both strategies certainly have merit, this is what Dr. Bernstein has written in *Rational Expectations: Asset Allocation for Investing Adults* regarding this choice.

> If you want to reduce your portfolio risk, it is far more efficient to simply substitute riskless assets for risky ones rather than try to inoculate your risky assets with other risky and non-correlating ones.

"What he is saying is that shifting a portion of the portfolio to the Foundation is choosing to **avoid** the risk altogether with those particular funds rather than attempting to **manage** the risk.

"Now, how much and when to shift to the Foundation must be customized to your own personal needs and will depend on many factors including, but not limited to, your personal comfort with risk, how much of your retirement income is dependent on your nest egg, and the timing of how soon you will be taking income from your nest egg. Don't worry, all of this will be discussed in greater detail before your own plan will be complete.

"Now, I'm sure Wall Street William was required to share with you the risks of investing in the stock market. However, Super Retirement Planner likes me to be very thorough, so let me share the following from Dr. Bernstein in *The Intelligent Asset Allocator: How to Build Your Portfolio to Maximize Returns and Minimize Risk*:

> So, how risky are stocks? Not so much for young savers and Three Mile Island toxic for older ones.

"In other words, the Foundation is important—especially during retirement. I hope this makes sense. Please let me know if you have any questions."

Once again, Jack and Jill looked at each other.

"I don't think so," Jack responded. "I am sure we are both curious to figure out how much we should be putting toward the Foundation and what types of accounts fit here other than savings and money market accounts."

Susan understood and nodded.

"Ah, yes, what exactly should you use to provide safety for your principal?

"As always, let's keep in mind our goal: my assumption here is that we are seeking to provide safety of principal, but we're willing to exchange time for a higher return or higher potential return." She then listed the most common solutions:

- FDIC-insured CDs
- Federally backed US bonds, notes, and bills
- Fixed and fixed indexed annuities

"Let's take a look at each of them," she said.

FDIC-INSURED CDS

"Historically, FDIC-insured certificates of deposit have been a great option to provide safety. They are typically anywhere from one to five years in length, so they don't require an unreasonable time commitment. The only downside is the same as the options for the emergency reserve: historically low interest rates.

"Most people approaching or in retirement have not been using CDs much simply because rates have been so poor for so long, and no one is predicting significantly higher rates anytime soon."

FEDERALLY BACKED US BONDS, NOTES, AND BILLS

"Even with our country's financial struggles, US government securities are generally considered to be the safest investments in the world. The reason is simple: to date, our government has never once defaulted on a commitment to pay for a security that it has issued, such as a bond, note, or bill. Of course, I'm sure you know that many people are very concerned about America's financial situation—specifically that we may spend $900 billion more than we take in this year and that the balance of our total debt is currently estimated to be more than $25 trillion!"[19]

Jack's face started getting red.

"Susan, if you want to avoid riling Jack up and getting sidetracked, we better move on to another topic!" Jill noted.

Susan had seen this reaction before. "Oh, I understand. We all know that we shouldn't spend more than we make, and yet here is our own government spending almost a trillion dollars more than we make in just one year!"

"Thank you! It's insane!" Jack was so happy to hear Susan agree.

"You're welcome."

Susan liked to show that she could empathize, and she also knew how to continue to move the conversation along.

"So these solutions are considered extremely safe. They're also somewhat accessible. They can typically be sold at any time, but it's very important to know that the value may be higher or lower than what you originally paid.

"As far as the biggest downside, once again, it's low current interest rates. You generally earn more interest when you commit your money for a longer period of time. But right now, ten-year

---

19 "Debt vs. Deficits: What's the Difference?" *Peter G. Peterson Foundation*, https://www.pgpf.org/blog/2016/10/debt-vs-deficits-whats-the-difference and https://www.usdebtclock.org/.

notes only pay less than 1 percent per year. And if that isn't bad enough, thirty-year bonds are currently paying less than 2 percent per year. The bottom line is, it's difficult to imagine a retiree using these successfully with rates as low as they are."

Jill summed up what they were all thinking.

"I understand why we need money in the Foundation. But it's tough to see how to make sure we never run out of money if we're not making *any* money on our money."

Jack nodded in agreement.

Susan smiled.

"I'm with you. Let's move on."

FIXED OR FIXED INDEXED ANNUITIES

"Let me start by saying there is probably not a more confusing term in all of finance than *annuity*. That is because if you asked one hundred people what they think of when they hear the word, you'll probably get one hundred different answers. Let me start by quickly addressing two types of annuities that do not fit as a solution for most retirees for one reason or another. It's my hope that this will help reduce any confusion."

ANNUITIES THAT DO NOT FIT MOST RETIREES
VARIABLE ANNUITIES

"These are typically used as a tool to help you invest your money for accumulation. It offers accounts that work very much like mutual funds. Some variable annuities may offer guarantees for your death benefit and even for income. However, at its base, the variable annuity is an investment.

"Please understand, I'm not saying it is necessarily bad. I'm just saying this means it doesn't fit into the Foundation. A variable annuity will generally fit in the Roof. So that is a discussion that is better had with Wall Street William.

"I bring this up for two reasons. The first is that these types of annuities typically have a number of layers of fees. If you Google 'annuity fees,' you get millions of articles on the subject. Generally, when you're discussing the high fees of annuities, this is the type that is being discussed.

"The second reason is, I run into all kinds of baby boomers who were sold variable annuities. Some of these annuities offer some kind of 'guarantee' of a certain percent per year. But the guarantee often has lots of fine print along with it. The bottom line is, if you *think* you have a guarantee on your annuity, you need to make *sure* that you really do. The last thing you can afford is to have a substantial amount of your nest egg tied up in one account and suddenly have less money or less income than you ever thought possible the next time the stock market sees a significant drop. Does that make sense?"

Jack and Jill nodded. Jill was frustrated.

"This is the kind of thing that makes all this so scary," she said. "How in the world are normal people supposed to be able to figure this stuff out? You get these booklets in the mail on your investments, and there's no way anyone can understand them. They're dozens or even hundreds of pages long, filled with fine print and legal and investment jargon that are impossible to decipher."

"Boy, you are so right," Jack added. "I like to think I'm pretty good with money and investments. But I tried to read past the first paragraph once, and it was all I could do to avoid falling asleep!"

"You're both right," Susan agreed. "It's not impossible to figure all this out on your own, but it is time-consuming and very difficult. But if you're working with Super Retirement Planner, then you don't have to worry about this. His team can look at what you have and figure out what it is, and review it with you in plain English.

"Remember, his team isn't necessarily for or against anything. So it doesn't matter what you have. They'll review it, place it in the appropriate level of the house, then help you determine if it is an appropriate solution for what you're trying to accomplish."

Susan could see the relief across Jack's and Jill's faces.

"Praise the Lord!" Jill replied. "I don't want to be responsible for all of this! And Jack, I love you and trust you, but honestly, I don't want you to be either!"

"I totally understand and am happy to 'retire' from the job!" Jack said with a smile.

Susan enjoyed the moment but only very briefly. She knew there was more work to be done.

"Very good, let's keep moving.

IMMEDIATE ANNUITIES

"I suggest that when you think of an immediate annuity, you think of a pension because they work in a similar way. With an immediate annuity, you invest a lump sum of money, and you immediately begin receiving income either for a set period of time or for life. Although lifetime income is certainly a good thing, immediate annuities are extremely limited, which is why they aren't used very often anymore.

"One problem is that in general, immediate annuities are irrevocable. This means that once you have placed your money there, there is no way to change the account. Also, depending on the type of immediate annuity, when you die, your beneficiaries may receive little or nothing. For these reasons, we believe there are typically much better annuity options, so we're going to move on to other types of annuities. Sound good?"

Jack and Jill nodded.

ANNUITIES THAT MAY FIT MANY RETIREES
FIXED ANNUITIES

"Another type of annuity is a fixed annuity. I think a good comparison of a fixed annuity is a CD," Susan said. "Although they are, of course, different, the goal of a fixed annuity is simply to pay you better interest than a savings account while keeping your money safe. Fixed annuity safety is based on the Legal Reserve System.

"This system requires that insurance and annuity companies have $1 in reserves for every $1 in benefits owed.[20] This means

---

20 https://annuity.com/how-safe-is-your-fixed-indexed-annuity/.

that if you go to your annuity company to cash out your annuity, they have to be able to fulfill that request. As you may already know, that is not the case with banks. Banks make money by taking in deposits and lending money back out. So they are not expected to keep $1 in reserves for every $1 of deposit.

"In fact, most highly rated and respected insurance and annuity companies maintain what is called surplus capital. This is the term for deposits above the required amount. Many of these companies maintain surplus capital of anywhere from 4 to 10 cents per reserve dollar."

Jack was impressed.

"Wow, backing my money more than dollar for dollar sure sounds good. It's too bad banks didn't do that back in 2008 when so many of them failed."

Susan had heard comments like this before and knew Jack needed a little more explanation.

"Jack, keep in mind that although I have great faith in the Legal Reserve System for annuities, it doesn't mean annuities are better than bank accounts. They're just different. Your bank accounts serve an important purpose for accessibility and flexibility that annuities typically do not offer. Plus, bank accounts are FDIC insured whereas annuities are not. Does that difference make sense?"

Jack nodded.

"Yes, it does. So what are the downsides to the fixed annuity?"

"Well, we just covered two of them: they are not FDIC insured, and they typically don't offer accessibility without penalties," Susan explained. "In fact, early withdrawal penalties can be quite high. So it's important that anything placed into a fixed annuity isn't needed for emergencies.

"The last downside to a fixed annuity is the same as bank accounts and US-backed securities: low current interest rates. These days, a fixed annuity may be offering around 3 percent interest per year. Even though that may be a little higher than CDs and savings bonds, it's still not enough for most people to live off in retirement."

"Yes, I agree that they sound safe, but it would be nice to be able to earn more on our money," Jill said with a sigh.

"That leads us into our next type of annuity," Susan said.

FIXED INDEXED ANNUITIES

"As you might guess from the name, this works a lot like the fixed annuity. The biggest difference is that instead of paying you a fixed interest rate, your returns are based on an index. When these were originally invented back in the 1990s, they were usually tied to the S&P 500, which is made up of the 500 largest public companies in the United States. As these have gained popularity with retirees, companies have developed various other indexes as well. But essentially, the idea is that you cannot lose principal, and you have the opportunity to earn better returns than CDs, savings bonds, and fixed annuities based on some kind of index tied to stocks, bonds, or a mixture of the two.

"So let's break these down with pros and cons." Then she began with the pros.

- Fixed indexed annuities fall under the Legal Reserve System, so you can consider your principal safe. Even if the index crashes, your principal should not be at risk.
- Upside potential: the different types of indexes and strategies on the market change from time to time. But using current assumptions, I believe that a fixed indexed annuity using the S&P 500 today could be reasonably expected to earn an average of 3 to 5 percent per year. If you're willing to consider different and newer types of indexes and different contract terms, I believe the average that could be expected could increase to 3 to 7 percent per year.

Now Jack was getting excited.

"Wow, 7 percent per year with my principal guaranteed—sign me up!"

Jill rolled her eyes.

"Honey," she said, "average up to 4 to 7 percent per year. That is a huge difference from saying that you will earn 7 percent per year!"

Jack paused, then smiled.

"Okay, I'll take a guarantee of 6 percent per year!"

Jill rolled her eyes again and playfully jabbed Jack in the arm. Susan appreciated Jill trying to set Jack straight.

"Okay, Jack, so let's make sure we're on the same page. Yes, fixed indexed annuities have some good features, but they definitely have cons, too. So let's make sure we cover those." She presented them as:

- There typically is no minimum interest-rate guarantee. This means that if the index you choose doesn't perform well, you may not earn anything that year.
- These are typically long-term contracts. The most competitive fixed indexed annuities typically have contract terms between seven to ten years long. Most companies allow you to withdraw a portion without fees or penalties each year, but you can't get all of your money out without penalty until the end of the contract.
- The index terms can and probably will change throughout the term of the contract. This is because of how the annuity company manages these accounts. In order to pay you interest based on an index, the annuity company is buying options on the index every year. If the cost of the options changes, that can affect the terms of what you might earn.

Jack shook his head.

"At first, it sounded too good to be true. Now it sounds like I'm going to tie up my money forever, and I'm not even going to make anything!"

"Jack, she specifically said she was going to cover the pros and the cons, and you didn't wait for the cons! Will you please just let her teach us?" Jill interjected.

Jack was frustrated, too. His was the worst kind of frustration: knowing that his wife was right and he was wrong!

"Thank you, Jill," Susan interjected. "Jack, you got excited and forgot there are no perfect investments! Everything has pros and cons. The bottom line is that the fixed indexed annuity isn't for everyone; it can be a good tool for someone who can allocate a portion of their nest egg long term, wants the peace of mind that their principal should be safe, and has the opportunity to earn more than CDs, savings bonds, and fixed annuities.

"I know that Super Retirement Planner will use them with clients who want part of their nest egg in the Foundation, and often they will plan to withdraw money out of the account systematically based on what they project it will return over the years."

Jack heard *systematic*, and his ears perked up.

"Wait a second. When you say 'systematic,' I begin thinking about the retirement villain Systematic Sammy, and I start to get nervous."

Susan was glad that Jack was still following along.

"Systematic Sammy is a huge risk to retirees, but he refers to taking income off an investment that can lose principal. Since we're dealing with a Foundation account, that risk doesn't apply here. Does that difference make sense?" When they nodded, she said, "Very good. Let's continue."

LIFETIME GUARANTEED INCOME

"The primary thing some people seek out with their Foundation allocation is guaranteed lifetime income. The reason is simple: the number one financial fear of Americans is running out of money.[21] The three possible sources to solving this fear include Social Security, pensions, and annuities that provide lifetime income guarantees.

"Use of guaranteed lifetime income annuities has increased dramatically in the last couple of decades. One likely reason for this is how uncommon pensions have become. There was a day when it was much more common for someone to work at the same place for most of their working career and retire with monthly pension income. Now those types of pension benefits are going the way of the dinosaur."

"Oh man, how nice would it be if we had a pension?" Jack interrupted. "Then we wouldn't have to worry about all this stuff!"

"That's true," Jill replied. "I guess we should be thankful that Social Security is still around."

"For now!" Jack was getting fired up again.

Jill knew Social Security was another hot button for Jack and quickly changed the subject.

"Okay, I am confused about one thing. I thought you told us that immediate annuities that pay income for life were *not* a good choice for most people. But now you're saying income annuities are much more common now. How can that be?"

"That's a great question actually," Susan replied. "Some kinds of fixed or fixed indexed annuities also offer a lifetime income

---

21   Edleson, Harriet. "Half of Americans Worry They Will Outlive Their Money." *AARP*, 21 May 2019, https://www.aarp.org/retirement/planning-for-retirement/info-2019/retirees-fear-losing-money.html.

guarantee. This structure typically avoids the two problems with immediate annuities. First, the income and withdrawal options are usually very flexible. You can decide when to start taking lifetime income as well as when you take other kinds of withdrawals.

"Second, these accounts generally pay the remaining account balance out to beneficiaries, so you don't have to worry about your family being left with nothing to show for your account. Do those differences make sense?"

Jill nodded. "Yes, that does sound far more appealing."

Susan jumped right back in.

"Yes, essentially, what some retirees have decided to do is to take a portion of their nest egg and create something like a 'personal pension.' There are obviously pros and cons to this type of strategy, and like other strategies, it's not for everyone. It is clearly a solution to the risk of outliving your money.

"As the study of retirement income planning has grown in the past couple of decades, researchers have decided time and again that this strategy can provide tremendous value and should be considered by more retirees."

WHAT THE HECK IS LMP?

"There is a technical term used in relation to this concept in the income planning community that you probably haven't heard before: liability matching portfolio. The concept suggests that while you're still working, it's logical to think of all of your investments in one pool or portfolio, but when you're retired, you should split your nest egg into two parts both figuratively and literally: one that will generate your income throughout retirement and another part essentially for everything else. The part of your nest egg that is set aside to create your retirement income is called your liability matching portfolio, or LMP.[22] I know that liability isn't a term most people throw around on a daily basis. Think of the total income you need your nest egg to create for you throughout your lifetime. That is the 'liability.' This idea 'matches' part of your portfolio to cover this expense.

"How important is it to consider your LMP during retirement? Listen to how Dr. Bernstein describes this concept in his book *The Intelligent Asset Allocator*:

> Your LMP, once achieved, should be sacred and should never, ever take a back seat to your desire for higher returns.

"Here's another related quote from Dr. Wade Pfau from *The Yin and Yang of Retirement Income Philosophies*:

> For retirees, the fundamental nature of risk is the threat that poor market returns will trigger a permanently lower standard of living. Retirees must decide how much risk to their lifestyle they are willing to accept.

"Let's think back to what we're trying to accomplish with our money," Susan stated. "Ultimately, why are you saving for retirement?"

Jack and Jill looked at each other.

---

22 M. Barton Waring and Laurence B. Siegel, "Don't Kill the Golden Goose! Saving Pension Plans," *Financial Analysts Journal* 63, no. 1 (January–February 2007): 31–45.

"I think we remember," Jill answered. "The purpose of saving for retirement is to make sure we never run out of money—that we're never old and broke."

Susan smiled.

"Very good. You are clearly good listeners."

Jack and Jill both had a look of satisfaction, as they already could tell that Susan didn't throw around compliments lightly.

"Your answer is exactly right," Susan continued. "We need to stop thinking of asset values and instead think about income.

"As I mentioned earlier, the only sources of income that provide guarantees are Social Security, pensions, and annuities. Since you can't allocate part of your nest egg to Social Security or pensions, that means each retiree needs to decide if a lifetime income annuity makes sense for them. Of course, that answer will vary wildly depending on each person or family's individual factors. Let me share one example of how someone might look at this from their perspective.

"Super Retirement Planner finds it very useful to calculate your GRIP. This stands for guaranteed retirement income percentage. This is a concept created by Dr. Pfau and refers to figuring out how much of your retirement income will have some sort of guarantee behind it." She quickly used a couple of examples:

A. Picture a couple who is about to retire, and they've determined they need $4,000 a month after tax to live off when they retire. Then they total up their combined estimated Social Security benefits and a pension and estimate that it will bring in exactly $4,000 a month after taxes. So their GRIP is 100 percent, which of course, is outstanding! Now, their income may not keep up with their expenses due to inflation, but they appear to be in great shape to begin their retirement. In their case, using an annuity to create guaranteed lifetime income may not make any sense.

B. Now imagine another couple getting ready to retire. They've calculated their after-tax needs in retirement to be $7,000 a month. But neither of them has a pension, and their total Social Security benefits only equal $3,500 a month. So their GRIP is only 50 percent. From this limited amount of information, it appears that they could benefit from considering allocating a portion of their nest egg toward a lifetime income annuity.

"Do both of those examples make sense?" she asked.

Before answering, Jill looked over at Jack and chuckled.

"Yes, Susan, those examples are great. I'm quite sure Jack is calculating our GRIP as we speak!"

Jack grimaced a little bit. "Yes, I don't have it exactly, but I think we are closer to 50 percent than 100 percent."

Susan had seen a similar look of worry on many people's faces before.

"Jack, make sure to look at the big picture. On the one hand, don't worry too much because that is the reason you've both saved your entire nest egg—to create income in retirement. On the other hand, it is good that you're realizing that there is a gap for your income that needs to be filled."

Jack listened intently.

"In other words, don't freak out about it, but don't get overconfident either."

"Actually, that's pretty good advice when it comes to retirement planning," Susan said with a smile. "Now, I'm sure you're wondering how we actually go about creating this guaranteed lifetime income. Over the last decade, the choice that has been growing in popularity is the fixed indexed annuity with a lifetime income rider. A rider simply means they're adding an income guarantee to the contract. Now, Jack, I'm sure you know by now that this is not a perfect annuity either."

Jack was caught off guard. Up until this point, she hadn't joked around, but he could see by the smile that she was just teasing, and he couldn't help but chuckle.

"Yes, if they're adding a lifetime income guarantee, there must be a catch or string attached, right?"

Susan nodded.

"Yes, exactly right. Essentially, most companies just add a fee onto the annuity for this lifetime income guarantee. I would sum this type of benefit up simply: if you're going to use the lifetime income guarantee, then the fee should not be a concern, but if you're not going to use the lifetime income guarantee, then you shouldn't be paying a fee for it!"

Jill smiled.

"That certainly makes good sense. So how do we know if we should add this rider or not?"

"Well, now you're getting over my pay grade," Susan replied. "That is a decision for you all in your planning with Super Retirement Planner. Now, let's quickly look at an additional reason many people allocate to the Foundation."

AN ADDITIONAL REASON SOME PLACE MONEY IN THEIR FOUNDATION
POTENTIAL ASSISTANCE WITH FUTURE LONG-TERM CARE COSTS

"In recent years, the long-term care insurance industry has faced a tremendous number of challenges which has rightfully caused concern for retirees as well as retirement planners. One solution that has been created is a Foundation account that potentially increases your income in times of nursing care need.

"Some of the options we've discussed today also offer this benefit. The most common example would be an annuity that offers you a lifetime income guarantee. When the account owner needs nursing care, depending on the company and the offering, the guaranteed income could increase for a set period. This increase would typically not be enough to pay for all the nursing care costs. But many find this option appealing, as they are attempting to reduce the risk of large, out-of-pocket nursing care costs while avoiding spending a fortune on long-term care insurance.

"Of course, not every Foundation offering provides this benefit, and each company will have its own limitations that you will want to make sure you understand. But generally speaking, does this make sense?"

"It does," Jill replied. "I'll never forget our discussion with Sarah Self-Pay regarding the risk and potential out-of-pocket costs due to nursing care."

Susan paused to take a close look at both Jack and Jill. She wanted to feel confident that they had followed everything she had shared and didn't have any pressing questions. She was pleased with how they had paid attention and felt good about their understanding.

"There you have it. We've covered everything that I believe is necessary for you to understand. Do you have any questions?"

Jack and Jill turned and looked at each other. They shook their heads.

"No, I think you've done a wonderful job," Jill replied. "We have a lot to think about."

Susan smiled again.

"Very well. I believe it's time to meet my friends for tea. I bid you farewell."

Suddenly, there was a puff of smoke. Predictably, once the smoke had cleared, Susan was gone.

"Even when you know it's going to happen, it is still surprising," Jill said with a laugh.

"You're right about that," Jack added. "And you're right that we have a lot to think about."

Editor's note: Because we are discussing specific offerings, compliance has asked us to add the following disclaimers related to annuities:

Annuities are long-term investments designed for retirement planning. Taxes may be due upon withdrawals from the contract. Withdrawals may be subject to a 10 percent federal penalty tax if made before age fifty-nine and a half and are subject to qualified retirement plan provisions. Withdrawals or surrenders may be subject to contingent deferred sales charges. Withdrawals can reduce the account value and the living and death benefits. Before deciding on an annuity, you should consider your income needs, risk tolerance, and investment objectives. Your investment professional can help you decide if annuities are a suitable investment and can help you choose an annuity.

Annuity contracts contain exclusions, limitations, reductions of benefits, and terms for keeping them in force. Investors should consider the contract and the underlying portfolios' investment objectives, risks, and charges and expenses carefully before investing. Please read the annuity prospectus for more complete information, including all charges and expenses before investing or sending money.

This is neither an offer nor a solicitation to purchase any products, which may be done only with a current prospectus. Investors should consider their investment objectives and risks, along with the product's charges and expenses before investing. Please read the prospectus carefully before investing.

SUMMARY OF MAJOR POINTS

- A Foundation account provides a guarantee of your principal and/or of a lifetime income guarantee.

- The most commonly used solutions are:
  - FDIC-insured bank accounts
  - Federally backed US bonds, notes, or bills
  - Principal and/or lifetime income guaranteed annuities
- Two types of annuities that don't fit for most retirees are variable annuities and immediate annuities.
- Two types of annuities that could fit for many retirees are fixed annuities and fixed indexed annuities.
- The primary reasons people allocate to the Foundation are:
  - Emergency reserve
  - Safety of principal
  - Guaranteed lifetime income
- LMP stands for liability matching portfolio and represents the part of your nest egg that is set aside to provide you with retirement income.
- GRIP stands for guaranteed retirement income percentage; you can calculate yours by dividing your guaranteed monthly income in retirement by the amount of income you seek.
- An additional reason Foundation accounts are used is for potential assistance with future long-term care costs.

Chapter 8

===

ENDOWMENT EDWARD

"Divide your portion to seven, or eight, for you do not know what misfortune may occur on earth."

—KING SOLOMON, ECCLESIASTES 11:2

Jack was standing at the refrigerator staring inside.

Jill walked up and chuckled.

"Are you waiting for something to jump out at you?"

Jack replied, "I'm trying to decide what we should do for lunch."

He shut the door. "We've learned so much already, I think I have all this retirement stuff bouncing around in my head, and it's making it difficult for me to focus on something simple like food!"

Jill gave Jack a hug. "I completely understand, and I know you're eager to meet our last mentor."

"Absolutely," Jack said. "It's been a couple of hours now since Susan left. I want to 'summon' our next mentor, but I don't know how to do it!"

Jill poured herself a glass of water. She couldn't remember seeing him so antsy.

"All right, well, let's think about what's left. We covered the Roof, which was for growth-oriented types of investments. We covered the Foundation, which was for options that provide some sort of safety. So what do you think fits in the middle?"

"I don't know!" Jack was flustered. "The only thing I can think of is way back when we met the retirement villains. Do you remember Antiquated Andy?"

Jill choked a little on her water from laughing.

"Are you serious? Are you asking me if I remember meeting and learning from a caveman? Of course, I remember him!"

Now Jack had to laugh.

"I'm sorry," he said. "I guess that was a stupid question. I just wonder if the Walls have something to do with what he talked about. You know, he explained that Wall Street has historically recommended stocks, bonds, and cash to individual investors, but he taught us about the potential benefits of investing like those universities that have billions invested. What were they called?"

"Endowments?" Jill asked.

At that very moment, another puff of smoke filled the room. As it started to fade away, Jack exclaimed, "Yes! We finally figured one out!"

Once the smoke dissipated, they could see their third and final mentor. "Hello, allow me to introduce myself. I'm Endowment Edward."

Jack and Jill looked him up and down. He looked completely different than their last two mentors. Young. Maybe in his early thirties with a boyish expression. He was dressed very simply in a plain blue T-shirt and jeans, with his hands in his pockets.

Jill blurted out, "Oh my goodness, you look exactly like that Facebook guy!"

"Yes, that's who I was trying to think of!" Jack agreed. "What's his name?"

"Mark Zuckerberg," Edward responded. "Yes, I can assure you I get that all the time."

"Yep, that's the guy!" Jill responded. "Well, welcome to our home. Can I offer you something to drink?"

Edward sat down at the kitchen table. "No, thank you. If you're both ready, I'm your last Blueprint Mentor, and I'm here to teach you all about the wonderful world of the Walls."

Jack and Jill scrambled to collect their notepads and pens and then sat down at the table as well.

"We're ready!" Jack promised.

WHAT ARE WALLS INVESTMENTS?

"Very well," Edward started. "First, many people think it's odd that we cover the Walls last. But it works out perfectly. You see, covering them last makes sense because the Roof and Foundation help define what the Walls are.

"Simply put, Walls investments are those that fit in between the Roof and Foundation. On the one hand, they strive to avoid the day-to-day swings of the stock market that affect so many Roof investments, but on the other hand, they are not guaranteed by FDIC, the US government, or any annuity and insurance company like the Foundation. Speaking of the stock market and bank accounts, that's a good time to mention Antiquated Andy."

Jack interrupted Edward because he was feeling quite smug. "Yes, actually, I was just bringing up Andy to Jill!"

Edward allowed a very small, wry smile. "Yes, I know. Anyway, Andy represents the old-fashioned suggestions from Wall Street, which haven't changed in more than a century: stocks, bonds, and cash.

"As you now know, stocks and bonds are in the Roof, and cash is in the Foundation. Although the Walls are not the same thing as endowment-style investing, they are related. You may recall that endowment-style investing gained popularity due to all of the biggest endowments adopting a similar approach.

"As a refresher, an endowment is essentially an investment fund that donors contribute to. However, rather than spending the donations, the endowment invests them and draws income from the investments. This is a very common approach used by universities and other nonprofit organizations. The person who initiated this movement was David Swensen, who has run the Yale endowment for more than three decades now.[23]

---

23   There are material differences between the terms under which endowments and individuals can invest in alternative investments. These differences include, but are not limited to, commissions and fees, conflicts of interest, access to investment opportunities, size, investment time horizons, and the ability to tolerate illiquidity. There is no standard or exact definition of the endowment model. Portfolio design, specific investments, and ultimately, performance vary considerably among endowments and investors. Kalos does not claim that any investor will achieve the same result as any endowment, institution, or other investor. Kalos's Investment Adviser Representatives have a conflict of interest when they recommend securities where they earn a commission as Registered Representatives of Kalos Capital. We address this conflict by disclosing the fees and commissions related to the investments recommended to our clients. Also, Kalos representatives do not earn both advisory fees and brokerage commissions on the same assets.

"You may remember Antiquated Andy sharing how well endowment-style investing has often performed. One example would be Yale's endowment. For the twenty years ending June 30, 2019, the performance has been 11.4 percent per year.

"During that time frame, the US stock market has averaged 6.4 percent per year, and the US bond market has averaged 4.9 percent per year. So if you compare the Yale endowment to a portfolio made up of 60 percent stock market and 40 percent bond market with a 1 percent annual fee, Yale's 11.4 percent per year makes quite a statement compared to the portfolio return of 4.8 percent per year."[24]

Edward had Jack's attention. "Holy cow, that's an insane difference—11.4 percent versus 4.8 percent!"

Jill was worried Jack would get carried away.

"Those are great returns, but honey, don't forget about the timeless truths that Super Retirement Planner taught us."

Jack looked at Jill and smiled.

"You're absolutely right." Then he turned and looked Edward square in the eye.

"All right, young man, what's the catch?"

Edward chuckled.

"Well, I certainly wouldn't call anything a 'catch.' But at the same

---

24 https://news.yale.edu/2019/09/27/
     investment-return-57-brings-yale-endowment-value-303-billion

time, I also wouldn't say Walls investments are perfect, as they are far from it. First of all, I've already explained that they're not guaranteed. So although managers of Walls investments are generally seeking to preserve principal, they can never guarantee it.

"I'll quickly mention one other tradeoff. Since these investments are not stocks, bonds, or cash, they are often referred to as 'alternatives.' Let me read this quote from the 2018 Yale Endowment Report:

> Alternative assets, by their very nature, tend to be less efficiently priced than traditional marketable securities, providing an opportunity to exploit market inefficiencies through active management. The Endowment's long-time horizon is well suited to exploit illiquid, less efficient markets.[25]

"In other words, some Walls investments are not always 'liquid' or available to sell. Now, of course, you wouldn't want all of your money tied up somewhere that you can't get to, but that is the beauty of the blueprint for your nest egg. No one puts all of it in the Walls. Does that make sense?"

"Yes, it does," Jack replied. "I could earn good returns, and the added diversification could lower the risk to my principal, but I may never be able to touch my money."

He smiled at Edward and Jill and finished.

"I'm just teasing. Yes, I understand that the tradeoff is that

---

25 https://static1.squarespace.com/static/55db7b87e4b0dca22fba2438/t/5c8b09008165f55d4b ec1a36/1552615684090/2018+Yale+Endowment.pdf.

you may have less access to withdrawing or switching the investments."

"Very good," Edward added. "A lack of ability to get into or out of an investment is a really important consideration. The downside is obvious: you may not be able to access that money when you want or need it. Interestingly, there is also a possible benefit. Listen to what Dr. Bernstein wrote in his book *The Four Pillars of Investing*. In the beginning of this quote, he is referring to fluctuations in the value of your home:

> It's a good thing that you can't check on its value every day or even every year. You happily hold on to it, oblivious to the fact that its actual market value may have temporarily declined 20 percent on occasion. Ben Graham observed this effect when he noted that during the Depression, investors in obscure mortgage bonds that were not quoted in the newspaper held on to them. They eventually did well because they did not have to face their losses on a regular basis in the financial pages. On the other hand, holders of corporate bonds, which had sustained less actual decrease in value than the mortgage bonds, but who supplied frequent quotes, almost uniformly panicked and sold out.

"So a lack of flexibility is definitely a negative aspect of an investment, but it can actually offer benefits as well. Now, I'm sure you're curious about the specific investments that fit into the Walls, but before digging into specific examples, I believe it's best to remember another timeless truth of beginning with the purpose of your money.

"Let's discuss the various reasons people may choose to allocate some of their nest egg to the Walls."

REASONS TO ALLOCATE TO THE WALLS
DIVERSIFICATION

"The first reason is simple: for diversification. I'm sure that Super Retirement Planner already shared that there is no such thing as a perfect investment, right?"

"Oh, yes," Jill responded. "That was very eye-opening and crystal clear."

"Very good," Edward continued. "And I know Super Retirement Planner also explained that the whole purpose of the blueprint for your nest egg is to help you diversify your money. Within the Walls, this is simply taken to the next level. You see, you should not have all your Walls money in one thing. Generally, most of Super Retirement Planner's clients have numerous different holdings within the Walls. So, in addition to the other reasons to use the Walls that we're about to get to, these holdings provide additional diversification. Does that make sense?"

Jack and Jill nodded in approval.

"Great, we'll continue."

AVOID DAY-TO-DAY MARKET SWINGS

"The second goal of allocating to the Walls is to seek to avoid the day-to-day swings of the stock market. Now, this is probably an obvious benefit to an investor, especially one close to or in retirement, but I argue that this has become far more important over the past generation or two.

"Think about how the stock market moved prior to cable news. How often were you able to keep up with the news?"

Jack laughed, thinking back to how things used to be.

"We either watched the evening news or read about it in the newspaper."

Edward nodded. "That's exactly right. If you wanted an update during the day, it would have had to come from listening to the radio. The news simply did not travel fast.

"Now think about how twenty-four-hour news channels changed things. First came CNN, then channels that focused specifically on money and investing that would even show the Dow Jones changing second by second. Suddenly, the frequency of information and news changed dramatically. Then, of course, you had the change caused by the internet, wireless connections, and all the 'smart' devices we have. Now if you want to catch up on the news, what do you do?"

Jill jabbed Jack's arm with her elbow.

"*Some* people are addicted to checking it on their phone!"

Jack smiled. This was not the first time they had this conversation. "She's right that I check it too often, but it is awfully nice to be able to access updates so easily."

Edward was glad they were both being so honest.

"Thank you, Jill. It absolutely can be an addiction. The speed of news also causes a complication for investors. Nowadays, just about anything can swing the stock market in one direction or the other.

"This is another reason why I can't imagine someone keeping their entire nest egg in the Roof. So Walls options seek to protect you from these swings as much as possible."

"Absolutely," Jack interjected. "If another 2008 happens, we need options to keep us from losing our minds!"

"Well, first of all, if we're talking about a large drop in the stock market, there definitely *will* be another 2008 someday," Edward corrected Jack. "We just don't have any idea of *when* that will happen, but you're right; investors need something not only to try to protect them from losing money, but they also need something to protect them mentally and emotionally."

"I'm sure Wall Street William explained one of the biggest problems with the Roof is that we just aren't wired to be able to handle those wild market swings. This leads most of us to make bad decisions. Therefore, *if* Walls investments can avoid or at least reduce those swings, that is a valuable addition to your allocation. Does that make sense?"

Jack and Jill looked at each other to make sure they were both following. They both nodded.

"As you might imagine, exactly how this works differs for each of the different Walls options, and I promise we'll get to that a little later. Now let's move on to the next point."

SEEK BACKING FOR PRINCIPAL

"The third purpose for someone to place funds in the Walls is because these investments are generally backed by something. Although stock market investments can lose most or even all their value in a day, most Walls investments are backed by something real, which can provide more stability.

"An example I like to use is Enron. Back in the 1990s, the stock market was booming. By the middle of 2000, the stock price reached a peak of $90.75. In fact, at that time, it was valued as the sixth most valuable company in the entire world! Take a look at this chart to see what happened next."[26]

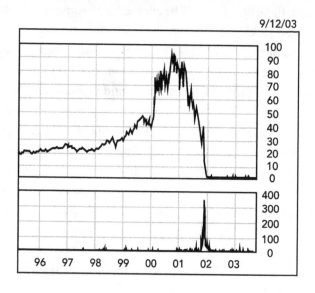

"Now, think about this for a second. We've all heard about stocks that go way up in value and then come crashing down, but I bet you don't ever think about it being one of the biggest, most respected companies in the world! And yet, that's exactly what happened. So how is this even possible? The reason is that a stock or bond is not really 'backed' by anything. A stock or bond is a security. That means the value can go way up, or it can go way down, including all the way down to nothing.

26 Segal, Troy. "Enron Scandal: The Fall of a Wall Street Darling." *Investopedia*, Investopedia, 22 Sept. 2020, Https://Investopedia.com/updates/enron-scandal-summary/.

"Imagine if someone recommended you invest in what they called a 'blue chip stock,' and you ended up losing all of your money over the course of a year or two."

Jack was getting angry again.

"That's insane! If one of the biggest stocks in the world can become worthless, what possible chance do regular people have of figuring this stuff out?"

"I completely understand how you feel," Edward said as he nodded. "This is just another example of why diversification is so important. It doesn't matter how much confidence you or your friend, or broker, or plumber, or anyone else has in one stock, you always have to remember that the investment *can* be lost.

"Now, let's use another example to show the difference of an investment in the Walls. Think of companies that have retail stores throughout the country. Let's use Walgreens as an example. If you own stock in Walgreens, it could do very well. But what if Walgreens were to go out of business? If you own the stock, what would happen?"

Jack was still fired up.

"You're in the same boat as the chumps who owned Enron. You lose all of your money," he ranted.

"Yes, you could lose all of your money," Edward replied. "Let's look at it a little differently. Instead of owning stock in Walgreens, what if you own the buildings that Walgreens rents? Now, what happens if Walgreens goes out of business?"

Jack was still upset from imagining losing his investment and couldn't think of an answer right away. Jill hesitated, then said, "Well, you still own the building, but if Walgreens is out of business, you're not getting any rent anymore."

"Very good, Jill," Edward replied. "It's certainly not great news for you because if Walgreens doesn't exist anymore, they certainly won't be paying you rent! But instead of losing everything, you still own the land and you still own the building. This is what we mean by being backed by something. This doesn't guarantee that you can never lose; it is simply another way to try to lower the risk of loss of your investment."

"I see," Jill said. "That's why this fits between the Roof and the Foundation. It tries to lower the risk compared to the Roof, but it isn't a guarantee like the Foundation. So it fits in the middle."

Edward smiled. "Jill, thank you. I couldn't have said it better myself!"

SEEK STEADY INCOME

"The next reason to consider allocating to the Walls is for those who are seeking income from their nest egg. As people planning for retirement, I'm sure you can imagine that this is often the primary reason people make use of the Walls. Safe Susan must have mentioned the benefits of using the Foundation for income. A lot of investors use the Walls for income as well. In comparison, Walls investments can often pay higher income than the Foundation, but unlike the Foundation, Walls investments don't have guarantees."

This really had Jack's interest, and he leaned forward.

"Edward, I've been so irritated by how unbelievably low interest rates have been for so long. What type of rate of income would be possible in the Walls?"

Edward smiled because he was expecting this question.

"Jack, I'll answer you, but please keep in mind that these are investments, so rates are always changing. Right now, there are a number of options in the Walls that are offering income around 5 or 6 percent per year."

This was music to Jack's ears. "Five or 6 percent per year without risking our money in the stock market? That's what we've been waiting for!"

Jill stopped Jack before he could go any further.

"Honey, don't forget the first timeless truth: There are no perfect investments."

Jack paused and then stared at Edward.

"All right, Edward, so what's the catch?"

Edward couldn't help but laugh.

"Jill, once again, thank you for keeping us on track. Anytime something sounds too good to be true, it means you haven't heard the whole story! With the Walls, keep in mind that these are investments, so nothing is guaranteed. Walls investments that offer income typically seek to keep your income at the same level at all times. However, that income could decrease, and even though it doesn't happen every day, it's possible that the income could stop altogether; this is because it's an investment and not a guaranteed offering like those in the Foundation.

"If you remember the examples Susan gave you, many retirees use Foundation accounts to cover all of their necessary expenses in retirement. Then, once those are accounted for, they may use Walls investments to support the rest of their lifestyle. But we are getting a little ahead of ourselves. Before we go further down this path, let's wrap up our five reasons some allocate to the Walls."

SEEK INFLATION PROTECTION

"I think this topic is quite simple: the goal here is to have some of your money avoid the potentially frequent ups and downs of the Roof but also offer more potential upside than what you could generate with money in the Foundation. Of course, since retirees face an unknown lifetime of income to generate, squeezing some returns out of your nest egg should be one of your goals.

"Does that make sense once again how it fits right between the Roof and Foundation?"

Jack and Jill nodded.

"That's great. I'm sure you're eager to hear more about what exactly these investments look like.

"Let's begin by digging into what these allocations are often invested in."

COMMON WALLS ALLOCATION OPTIONS
REAL ASSETS

"This is one of the most striking differences between how endowments and most individuals invest," Edward began. "Endowments often allocate the largest percentage of their portfolio to real, tangible assets, otherwise known as 'hard assets.' In contrast, most individual investors don't have *any* of their nest egg invested here.

"The obvious question is, why do endowments often direct a large portion here? Who is better to answer this question than the man who has run the Yale endowment since 1985? This is what David Swensen wrote in his acclaimed book *Pioneering Portfolio Management*:

> The real assets category includes real estate, oil and gas, and timberland, which share the common characteristics of sensitivity to inflationary forces, high and visible current cash flow, and opportunity to exploit inefficiencies. Real assets provide attractive return prospects, excellent portfolio diversification, and a hedge against unanticipated inflation.

"Mr. Swensen tends to write in a very technical way, so let's break this quote down one step at a time.

"The first reason many investors appreciate real assets is for cash flow. Think back to that Walgreens building again. If Walgreens is still in business, then we're getting rent payments from them each and every month. That is valuable to any investor, but of course, especially to retirees.

"Next up is added diversification. Real assets and the stock market often move in different ways and at different times. This provides tremendous value and comfort to investors. Now, of course, this works better at some times than others. The year 2008 was an example of when it didn't work well since the stock market *and* real estate were both hit hard. Please keep in mind that although we believe diversification is quite valuable, it doesn't actually guarantee anything.

"Finally, real assets provide a hedge against inflation. I personally think this is quite interesting. As you probably remember from when you met the Invisible Enemy, inflation can be a daunting villain for retirees. When your living expenses are increasing, that puts more pressure on your nest egg, and this challenge is compounded because some investments like stocks and bonds don't always perform well if there is a lot of inflation.

"Thankfully, investments like real estate work very differently. You see, real estate often increases in value with inflation due to the fact that the cost of constructing a new building would be increasing as well. As lifestyle costs go up, so do building costs such as labor and materials. This refers to a building's replacement cost. The bottom line is that in times of higher inflation, the strong relationship between replacement cost and market value could help your real estate investments perform quite well.

"Let me stop there and see if all of that makes sense."

Jack and Jill looked at each other, then Jack spoke first.

"Yes, it makes so much sense. I think what took me a few minutes was to change my thinking about real estate. When I think about real estate, I'm normally thinking about our home. But I have to remember to instead think about things like your Walgreens example. When you talk about what it costs to replace a piece of real estate, that's not anything we ever think about with our home. But it definitely makes sense with the Walgreens building. If it costs way more to build a new Walgreens building, that is going to naturally make the value of your building increase."

"Oh, that's a great way of explaining it," Jill interjected. "Nicely done!"

Jack smiled at Jill and looked over at Edward to see if he approved as well.

"Yes, that is an excellent clarification. The majority of savers and investors have only one real estate 'investment,' which is their home. But your home should always be considered a place to live more than an investment. That is a good distinction that we're talking about something different now.

"Let's go down that path and focus specifically on real estate."

REAL ESTATE

"When we talk about investing in real estate in the Walls, we're not talking about your home, and we're not talking about buying a house, fixing it up, and flipping it or any other kind of residential real estate. Rather, we're talking about the world of commercial real estate.

"It's helpful to understand that most large companies actually don't want to own their real estate. For example, Starbucks owns very few of their more than 29,000 stores, and 7-Eleven actually doesn't own a single one of their more than 68,000 locations worldwide. That means someone else owns those stores and collects rent from those companies.[27]

"Of course, commercial real estate is far more than retail stores like these. Other examples of commercial real estate include distribution centers for companies like Amazon or Walmart, apartment complexes, hotels, and office complexes.

"The most common approach to investing in commercial real estate is to buy a portfolio of these types of assets, collect rent—which is paid out to investors as dividends—then attempt to manage the portfolio to hopefully increase the overall value over time.

"Does that help explain real estate investing in the Walls?"

"Yes, definitely, thank you," Jack replied. "I like the idea of collecting rent from Starbucks. It would be nice to take money from them for a change instead of giving it to them!"

Jack and Jill shared a hearty laugh knowing how much they have spent at Starbucks over the years.

"That's a great way to look at it," Edward said.

Edward didn't laugh often but had to smile at Jack's comment. "Now, let's look quickly at a second type of real asset."

---

27 "Starbucks TENANT OVERVIEW." *Net Lease Advisor,* https://www.netleaseadvisor.com/tenant/starbucks-coffee/.
"7-Eleven TENANT OVERVIEW." *Net Lease Advisor,* https://www.netleaseadvisor.com/tenant/7-eleven/.

OIL AND GAS

"Oil and gas can be a controversial topic due to arguments over global warming, so I will make this quick. If you aren't opposed to it, investing in oil and gas is another way to attempt to generate income while diversifying into yet another area. Although you may not pay close attention to it, I can say that oil prices and the stock market often move in completely different directions. So this is another way to diversify your portfolio."

Jill wanted to make sure she responded first.

"Yes, that makes sense. I'm sure none of us want to get off track, right?"

Jack simply nodded and smiled.

"Great!" Edward said. "Should we move on to a completely different type of investment in the Walls?"

"Wait," Jack jumped in. "I'm sorry to interrupt, but you've mentioned the terms *real assets* and *hard assets*. Is this where investing in gold would go?"

"Ah, now, that is a *great* question!" Edward always appreciated thoughtful questions.

"Yes, gold is certainly a hard asset. However, we would always consider gold an investment that fits into the Roof. Can either of you guess why?"

"I guess that would be because the price can change day by day?" Jack replied.

"Correct." Edward was glad Jack understood the reason right away. "In fact, gold prices can fluctuate dramatically—even minute to minute. Gold is kind of a fascinating investment. On the one hand, it does provide excellent diversification from things like stocks. On the other hand, the price can move a lot in a short time. There is also one downside of gold that is often overlooked: it doesn't provide income! If you buy a gold bar as an investment, it doesn't earn anything—it just sits there."

"Ah, yes, that's interesting," Jack said. "So it is another way to diversify, but unlike oil and gas and real estate, it doesn't actually 'do' anything. Thanks, that's very helpful."

Jill joined Jack in nodding. "I've heard people talk about investing in gold and have never understood it. But that actually makes a lot of sense to me."

Jack had one more thing that still didn't make sense.

"You mentioned that gold fits in the Roof because the price fluctuates, but doesn't the price of oil fluctuate just as much? Yet you're including it in the Walls."

Edward was impressed.

"Jack, that is a great catch. We touched on oil and gas only briefly. When I'm referring to oil and gas, I'm not referring to a public company like Exxon. I'm referring to a private company that manages oil and gas investments. Since the company is private, it would not be revaluing its investments daily.

"To be clear, a significant change in oil prices may very well affect the value of your investment, but I would still include this type of investment in the Walls because the private nature of the investment is attempting to shelter you from frequent price changes. Also, the management company will often hedge the portfolio against significant price changes. Even with the shocking oil price crash in early 2020, it was possible for some of these private portfolios to perform well.

"Even though oil and gas investments can provide a lot of benefits, I would consider it riskier than many other Walls investments because of how it can be affected by significant changes in oil prices. Does that help?"

Jack and Jill nodded.

"Terrific. Now let's jump into another area of the Walls."

SECURED PRIVATE DEBT

"In addition to real estate, one of the more common areas of investing in the Walls is called secured private debt. Although that's probably not a name that you've heard very often or ever, it's actually a pretty simple idea. If you think of investing in a bond from a company, you are essentially lending money to that company. For example, in August 2020, Google's parent company Alphabet issued $10 billion in bonds of various lengths of time.[28]

"Because of their size and stability, investors generally considered these bonds to be reasonably low risk. Since you know that risk and return are related, that means the returns are not very

---

28 "Alphabet Borrows $10B with Focus on Sustainability Bonds - 9to5Google." *Google*, Google, https://9to5google.com/2020/08/03/alphabet-borrows-10-billion-with-focus-on-sustainability-bonds/.

high. For example, the ten-year Alphabet bond was returning 1.1 percent per year."

"Wait." Jack had a look of disgust on his face. "I'm committing my money for ten years, and all I'm getting is 1.1 percent per year?"

"Correct," Edward nodded. "Now, let's remember the pros and cons of a Roof investment like this. The pro is that there is a market for Alphabet bonds, so at any time during the ten years, you can sell your bond. The con is that the price of that bond can fluctuate during that time, so you don't have any guarantee that you would get back what you paid for it. Although today we think Alphabet is a company that will be here for a long time, in the unlikely event that they would go bankrupt during the next ten years, it's possible that you could lose all of your money."

Jack shook his head again.

"So I get a terrible return and could lose all of my money. Gee, thanks."

Edward cracked another smile. He couldn't help but appreciate Jack's sarcasm.

"That's actually well said, Jack. That relationship is why I'm sure Wall Street William mentioned that such highly respected people as David Swensen and Warren Buffett don't recommend bonds for individual investors.

"So what does all of this have to do with the Walls? Bonds are a way to lend money to a public company like Alphabet. Secured private debt is a way of lending money to a private company. Let's break down the differences.

"First, private companies don't issue bonds. When they are looking to grow, they have to borrow. So a secured private debt portfolio manager would build a portfolio of loans to various companies.

"Second, I often get asked about the types of companies that borrow. It is a wide range. Many portfolio managers say they target companies with revenues between $10 million and $1 billion per year. These companies can be in all types of industries.

"Third, since private companies are not traded on the stock market, in general, that means these loans can be less volatile than bonds like Alphabet's. The good news is that this may provide stability. The bad news is that it may be more difficult to sell this investment.

"Fourth, the investor protection tends to be much different than with bonds. As I mentioned, if Alphabet were to go bankrupt, the bond investor could lose all their money. However, with a 'secured' loan, the company is willing to put up collateral to back the loan. Just like when you put up your house to get a mortgage, these companies have to put something up to help protect your investment.

"Now, this doesn't guarantee to protect your principal, but it simply adds a layer of protection in case the company has financial difficulties.

"Last but not least, these loans are often set up with variable interest rates. This could prove to be beneficial in today's historically low interest rates. If interest rates do increase in the coming years, we could see the rates on our investments rise as well.

"To summarize, secured private debt is designed to generate

income, provide additional diversification, and attempt to preserve your original principal. Do you have any questions?"

Jack, as usual, was most interested in returns.

"What type of income rate are we talking about? I sure hope it's better than 1.1 percent per year!"

Edward smiled. "Of course, rates and income can change, but right now, these rates are generally more than 5 percent per year. Keep in mind, these are typically not designed for growth. They are simply another way to generate income."

"Heck, it's awfully tough to find 5 percent these days, so that does sound interesting," Jack mused. "So what does this type of investment look like? I'm assuming you're not picking one company and loaning to them?"

"You're exactly right," Edward replied. "Although there are different ways to invest in this area, the most common right now is through various types of funds. Generally, this means that the funds would be invested in numerous different companies to provide additional diversification. Even though the goal is to preserve principal, the share price would fluctuate as often as daily, and the type of fund would determine how often you can access your investment. Quarterly is a common option. That would mean that you would have the ability to redeem shares every ninety days."

Jack nodded in understanding. "My only other question is, are there any other downsides to this type of investment?"

Edward paused. "Well, yes, now that you mention it. Due to

current regulations, even though these loans are to private companies, Super Retirement Planner has found that the valuations are not as stable as other Walls investments. In the short run, this particular option might have more variations in its value.

"Now let's quickly look at one final area of the Walls."

REAL ESTATE DEBT

"We've talked about investing in real estate, and we've talked about lending money. If you put those two together, another similar area of the Walls is lending money for real estate investments. Just like we talked about when we covered real estate, we're not talking about people's homes; we're talking about commercial real estate.

"Although some commercial real estate investors may pay cash, others will invest a down payment and borrow the rest. As a Walls investor, you can allocate part of your funds toward lending on these transactions. As you might imagine, the building itself is the collateral. Simply speaking, we would want to consider investments here where the investor is making a sizable down payment to try to protect your principal. Just like with Secured private debt, with these investments, we're seeking income, diversification, and preservation of your original principal. Rates of return are often similar to secured private debt, and since the investment itself is different, this can provide additional diversification. Any questions on this option?"

Jack and Jill looked at each other, then shook their heads.

PUTTING IT ALL TOGETHER

"Excellent," Edward continued. "Let's put this all together. Super

Retirement Planner will spend much more time with you on how you decide how to allocate your nest egg, but generally speaking, most Walls investors are going to try to divvy their Walls allocation into a variety of these options. The goal isn't to pick the 'one' perfect option because, of course, you know that there is no such thing! Rather, the goal is to invest in a variety of these options and to hopefully provide you with diversification, income, and lower risk of principal loss than other types of investments that fall into the Roof.

"I'll share another way of saying it. Listen to how Bob Rice describes this in his book *The Alternative Answer*."

> Smart portfolios today must be panoramic and risk-tolerant. A panoramic portfolio reaches across a wide spectrum of assets, strategies, and time horizons to achieve higher current yields and more long-term growth.
>
> A risk-tolerant portfolio is like a fault-tolerant building: it can absorb major shocks without collapsing. Such stability requires active risk management to guard against sudden stock market declines; "uncorrelated" positions that generate returns independent of one another in typical business cycles; and "absolute diversification" so that strategies do not share a single point of failure in a crisis.

"I do have one more question," Jack said. "You've mentioned that Walls investments can be illiquid or difficult or impossible to sell. Can you explain that more?"

"Ah, yes, thank you for asking," Edward replied. "Your ability to get into and out of a Walls investment depends completely on the structure of the investment itself. Some Walls investments will provide quite a bit of flexibility. Think of the secured private debt examples we just talked about that allow you to sell shares every ninety days.

"However, other Walls investments will require you to commit to a much longer period. This can vary greatly depending on the investment itself. I'll use five years as a simple example. A portfolio manager may ask you to commit that portion of your nest egg allocation for five years to allow them the time to manage the portfolio.

"The question that might come to mind right away is, why would I give up control of my money for so long? The portfolio manager may have a good reason. Perhaps the goal is to strive to grow your principal over those five years. It is up to you and Super Retirement Planner to determine if that makes sense or not.

"Finally, it is up to you and Super Retirement Planner to decide how much of your Walls make sense being more tied up and how much makes sense to be easier to get into and out of."

Jack appreciated this explanation and, in a rare occurrence, didn't immediately have a sarcastic response.

He simply said, "Thank you."

"Yes, thank you so much," Jill added. "This was so interesting. I think Jack will agree that this was an area we really didn't know much about, and I can see why a retired person or someone close to retirement would find these options appealing."

"I couldn't agree more," Jack said. "Thank you very much for all of your time and expertise!"

Edward smiled one last time.

"That is very kind, and you are both so welcome. I am happy to say that you have now officially completed your time with your three retirement mentors. I guess you can now consider yourselves graduated!"

With his last words, one final cloud of smoke suddenly appeared. Jack and Jill found themselves doubled over, coughing and covering their mouths. When the smoke cleared and they looked up, Edward was gone.

"Well, that was really helpful and interesting," Jack said. "But now what do we do?"

Just then, their phone rang.

"I think we're about to find out!" Jill replied.

SUMMARY OF MAJOR POINTS

- Walls investments are those that fit in between the Roof and Foundation. They strive to avoid the day-to-day swings of the stock market, but they are not guaranteed by FDIC, the US government, or any annuity and insurance company.
- The reasons some allocate to the Walls are:
  - To diversify
  - To avoid day-to-day swings
  - To seek backing for principal
  - To seek income
  - To seek inflation protection
- The main areas of Walls investments are:
  - Real assets: real estate

- Real assets: oil and gas
- Secured private debt
- Real estate debt

Chapter 9

====

YOUR NEST EGG BLUEPRINT

"Let them criticize; let us sleep."

—DR. DAVID BABBLE, PROFESSOR EMERITUS, WHARTON
SCHOOL OF FINANCE, WHEN TOLD PEOPLE DISAGREED
WITH HOW HE PLANNED FOR HIS OWN RETIREMENT

Their morning started off like it typically did. Once again, Jack, Jill, their collie, Lassie, and two cups of coffee all gathered on their back porch.

Like most mornings, Jill began the day's conversation. "Well, today's the day! Are you excited?"

"Oh, yes, you know that I am," Jack said with a chuckle. "I don't know exactly what we're going to learn from Super Retirement Planner today, but I am hoping it's going to give me a lot of peace of mind about when I can retire and how we will actually do it."

Jill sipped her coffee and nodded.

"Yeah, it's kind of crazy to think about all the things that brought us here. First, we moved to Metropolis. Then we found our church. Then we met Dick and Jane at the get-together. After that, we met—in order—seven retirement villains, Super Retirement Planner, and finally, the three Blueprint Mentors. On the one hand, it seems like it took forever. On the other hand, I can't believe we've done so much!"

"You're right. It is amazing to think back to how things happened," Jack concurred. "I'm relieved that I'm not trying to figure all of this out on my own anymore, and I hope that having help puts you at ease, too."

"It does," Jill responded. "You know it wasn't an insult to you. I just knew that planning retirement isn't your area of expertise."

"Yes, of course I understand," Jack said with a smile.

He took another sip of his coffee. "Now, do you have our notepads ready?"

Jill took a final swig of coffee and stood up.

"Notepads and pens are ready. Let's go!"

* * *

Super Retirement Planner entered the conference room and shook hands with Jack and Jill.

"It's great to see you again. So tell me, what did you think of the three Blueprint Mentors?"

As they all sat down at the table, Jack chuckled. "They were really great. I would say they were enlightening."

"I'm glad to hear that," Super Retirement Planner said with a smile. "I'm curious. What exactly do you mean by enlightening?"

Jack paused and considered the question he hadn't expected.

"Well, let me see. I think before we met the mentors, neither of us really had any idea how you could retire off your nest egg. Now that the mentors have explained how to use the three levels to divvy up our nest egg, I think we understand the basic options that we can use and how they all work together.

"Of course, now we're ready for you to show us how to design *our* blueprint!"

"That's great, Jack. Thank you," Super Retirement Planner replied. "Jill, is there anything you would add to that?"

"No, I don't think so," Jill responded. "Jack and I have been talking about everything ever since we met the first retirement villain. He's right. We went into this process unsure of how to retire. Although we still don't know all of the details, we feel a lot better about how much we understand and where we are going."

"Excellent!" Super Retirement Planner said. "Well, then, I see you have your notepads ready. Shall we jump into it?"

Jill grabbed her pen. "Sounds good!"

"Just like the other areas we've covered, we are going to begin with some important principles," Super Retirement Planner began.

"As you know, we believe that you have to have a structure to think about such important topics. For actually designing your blueprint, we have three rules."

THE THREE RULES OF DESIGNING YOUR BLUEPRINT
1. FIRST AND FOREMOST, FOCUS ON YOUR GOAL

"Once again, we have to always remember to focus on your goal: what is the purpose you are working toward? Jill, you just said it short and sweet: to retire without worrying about running out of money. That is the primary purpose for most of our clients, and I would wager it is the primary purpose for millions of baby boomers right now!"

Jack and Jill nodded in agreement.

2. TAKE AN AGNOSTIC VIEW

"The next rule to designing the blueprint for your nest egg is that it's important to truly consider all of the investment options that are available. Let me read this from Wade Pfau's book *Safety-First Retirement Planning*:

> Approach retirement income tools with an agnostic view. We must step away from the notion that either investments or insurance alone will best serve retirees.

"Remember, in our previous meeting when we talked about how a bias can significantly affect investment recommendations? It is important to remember that if our goal is to create the best possible allocation for you, we want to be able to consider all options available."

"I don't think either of us looks at any types of investment options as a religion we 'believe' in," Jack said. "We just want to use options that help us meet our goals."

Super Retirement Planner laughed a little bit. "You said, 'Meet our goals.' Jack, it sounds like you're quoting one of our timeless principles. Nicely done!"

Jack smiled and looked at Jill, who rolled her eyes back at him.

"But seriously, I couldn't have said it better myself," Super Retirement Planner continued. "Let's move on to the third rule."

3. YOUR BLUEPRINT MUST BE DESIGNED JUST FOR YOU

"The last point is a big one: we believe that as someone gets close to retirement, it's critical that the blueprint for your nest egg needs to be designed specifically for you. You see, we live in the information age, and any of us can use Google to try to find out anything that we want. Thousands or millions of authors online are happy to tell you how everyone should invest their money, but the truth is that we are all different for a number of reasons. We believe that as someone gets closer to retirement, we need to custom-build their blueprint based on a number of reasons."

WHY YOUR BLUEPRINT MUST BE DESIGNED SPECIFICALLY FOR YOU
WHICH INVESTING PHASE ARE YOU IN?

AND HOW CLOSE TO RETIREMENT ARE YOU?

"One item that must be considered: which investing phase are you in, and how close to retirement are you? As you might imagine, someone who is thirty should almost always have a different allocation than someone who is sixty, but it's also true that someone who is sixty and planning to retire at sixty-seven may have a very different blueprint for their nest egg from someone who is sixty and planning to retire next week. So where we are in the time of our lives is a huge consideration."

"That makes total sense," Jack concurred. "I wasn't really too concerned with our allocations in our thirties and forties, but I sure am now!"

"I always wondered if we were doing the right thing," Jill added. "But it has been only the last few years when I knew that we needed to somehow figure it out!"

"You both are making complete sense," Super Retirement Planner replied.

WHAT IS YOUR GRIP?

"The next reason that your blueprint must be designed specifically for you is that everyone approaches retirement with a different GRIP. As I know Safe Susan explained, this stands for guaranteed retirement income percentage, and it can have a substantial effect on how you divvy up your nest egg.

"Someone who is able to cover all their monthly needs with their Social Security and pensions will likely have a very different blueprint from someone who needs to use their nest egg to create most of their retirement income. Does that make sense?"

"Yes, their situations are completely different, so it makes sense that the right choice for each of them may be completely different, too," Jill responded.

"That's right, Jill," Super Retirement Planner replied. "This is an example of why we sometimes get aggravated when we hear someone saying that a particular investment or allocation is 'best' for everyone when we know there is no such thing!"

MAKE SURE YOUR ALLOCATION MATCHES YOUR COMFORT WITH RISK

"The next difference is one that is foundational to our beliefs, which is that you must make sure that your allocation matches your comfort with risk. You see, the world of investing is filled with people who write about the 'best' ways to invest. These theories are often based on long-term averages that show how great the stock market performs over time and often tries to shame all of us for not putting our money into more aggressive investments.

"But the truth is that the high returns mentioned aren't realistic for almost all of us. If the stock market drops 20, 40, or 60 percent, how many of us can ignore it and continue on with our lives without any worry or stress?"

"Not me!" Jack interjected.

"Not me either!" Super Retirement Planner agreed. "Listen to what William Bernstein wrote in one of his later books *The Investor's Manifesto*:

> Successful investing requires a skill set that very few people possess. This is difficult for me to admit; after all, I have written two books premised on the idea that anyone, given the proper tools, can turn the trick. Once again, I was wrong. Having emailed and spoken to thousands of investors over the years, I have come to the sad conclusion that only a tiny minority will ever succeed in managing their money even tolerably well.

"You see, Bernstein was extremely savvy and studied the math of investing to determine what types of investing strategies made the most logical sense. But over the years, he realized that the mental and emotional side of investing was much more important.

"The bottom line here is this: It's incredibly valuable for us to build an allocation that you are comfortable with. Not only do we want it to provide you with great peace of mind, but we also need to find a plan that you can stick with. Ultimately, one of the goals of the blueprint for your nest egg is that it gives you a strategy for dealing with times when the economy or the stock market is struggling. Here is one final quote of Dr. Bernstein's from *The Intelligent Asset Allocator: How to Build Your Portfolio to Maximize Returns and Minimize Risk*:

> Investing is a psychological game. A suboptimal strategy you can live with and execute is better than an optimal one you can't.

"I'll give you a quick example of what I mean. We have a client whom we've helped for a few years now. Before she hired us, she was talking to one of the biggest money managers in the country. She was about to retire and was really concerned with what to do with her nest egg. This money manager gave her a proposal that was invested half in the stock market and half into the bond market.

"She responded to them that she was concerned about having half of her money in the bond market because interest rates were so low, and she didn't feel like that would provide enough return for her. They came back to her with their solution: to put her entire nest egg into the stock market right before retirement!"

Jack's and Jill's jaws dropped.

"That just sounds crazy to me," Jill commented. "I doubt I would even be able to sleep at night."

"You're right," Jack added. "I think you would be lying awake wondering if the next crash was coming soon, and if it did, what we would have to do to make up for all the lost money."

"There may be people who are comfortable having their entire nest egg in the stock market in retirement, but I don't think I've ever met them!" Super Retirement Planner concurred.

"Is it kind of like when you said a few minutes ago about being agnostic?" Jill asked. "It's not that the stock market itself is bad, but you need to use stock market investments in a way that makes you comfortable. Does that make sense?"

Super Retirement Planner smiled and looked over at Jack.

"She's good! Yes, Jill, that's right. The stock market isn't bad.

However, it does expose us to risk, so we need to use it properly and carefully, especially as we get closer to retirement."

"Okay, so now that we've covered our principles, are you both ready to discuss how we design your blueprint?"

Jack leaned forward and held his pen hovering over his notepad.

"Are you kidding me? This is what I've been waiting for!"

Super Retirement Planner smiled. "Let's do it!"

HOW TO DESIGN YOUR BLUEPRINT
LAY OUT ALL OF YOUR MATERIALS

"The first step is to lay out all of your materials. That is simply an analogy for figuring out all of the resources you have to help you build your retirement plan. When most people hear this, they think only of their nest egg. But there are all kinds of resources that you might have. We're going to cover a pretty thorough list. Some people find this a little tedious, but it is really valuable to review all of the various resources that you have. Let's go through this list." He rattled them off:

- Human capital
  - Continuing career
  - Part-time work
- Home equity
- Financial assets
- Insurance and annuities
- Social capital
  - Social Security
  - Medicare

- Company pensions

"The first thing I'll clarify is that I've found that the term *human capital* is not one that most people use in day-to-day conversation! All it means is that your ability to work and earn income is an asset. It is an asset as long as you continue at your current jobs, and if either or both of you decide you want to work part time during retirement, that is an asset as well."

"Yes, I don't think either of us thought of it that way," Jill responded, "but it makes sense that it's an asset since it could help us cover the cost of retirement."

"That's right," Super Retirement Planner agreed. "Have you discussed if you would want to work part time or not?"

Jack and Jill looked at each other and chuckled.

"I don't think either of us really knows," Jack answered. "I think we would like to see if we can build a retirement plan assuming we don't ever go back to work. But if one or both of us may decide we would like to continue doing something, then that extra income is just gravy."

"I completely get it," Super Retirement Planner said. "Neither of you has ever retired before, so we don't expect you to be able to figure out exactly what is going to happen and exactly what you're going to want to do ahead of time. So we will build the plan that way.

"Let's move on to the next category, which is home equity. This certainly may not be spent for your retirement, but we do want to review all of your assets. So what is a rough guess at the value of your home, and do you have a mortgage?"

"I was definitely wondering about why that was on the list," Jill replied. "A rough guess is that our home is worth about $350,000. I'm thrilled to say that we don't have a mortgage anymore. It has always been my dream to have our home paid for. We worked at paying down the balance for years, and when we moved to Metropolis, we were finally able to do it!"

"Congratulations!" Super Retirement Planner said. "I know from doing this for a long time that having your home paid for is good financially as well as mentally and emotionally! Okay, that brings us to financial assets."

Jack began flipping through his notepad.

"Yes, I have that right here. My 401(k) has $800,000. Jill has an old 401(k) with $400,000 and an IRA with $200,000. We also have savings of about $100,000."

"Tell me about your savings," Super Retirement Planner replied. "Is all of that set aside for emergencies and retirement? Or do you have anything else in mind like buying a new car or doing a home remodel or something like that?"

"No, that is our emergency reserve, and it has been building up," Jack replied. "Since we paid off the mortgage, we've had extra money each month. It has been sitting in the savings account because we didn't know what to do with it."

"I completely understand," Super Retirement Planner responded. "By the way, I'll make a quick point related to your nest egg. Although we are designing your blueprint, don't worry about what type of account your money is currently sitting in. Most of the time, there are very few issues or limitations to allocating your 401(k), IRA, and savings accounts. We will review those accounts before making any changes, but that is something we will dig into after today. Does that make sense?"

Jack and Jill nodded, so Super Retirement Planner continued.

"Okay, the next category is insurance and annuities. Tell me about any life insurance or annuities you might have."

Jack paused. "Well, we don't have any annuities. The only life insurance we have is mine at work, and that goes away when I retire."

"I had asked Jack about that," Jill added. "Do you think we should have life insurance anymore?"

"It's a really good question," Super Retirement Planner replied. "That will be part of our analysis. Generally, as we get older, your assets are hopefully increasing, and your debts are decreasing, so your need for life insurance should be going down. But when we build your retirement income plan, we can also test for what would happen if one of you passed away to make sure you are protected.

"Okay, then the last section is social capital, which includes Social Security benefits, Medicare, and any pensions. Let's start with your Social Security estimates at full retirement age as well as any pension estimates you might have."

Jack scanned his notepad again. "Yes, I have all of that here. My Social Security estimate is $2,000 a month, and Jill's is $1,500 a month. She also has a pension from the state with an estimate of $500 a month from her years as a teacher."

"What about how exactly to take Social Security?" Jill asked. "I've heard that is one of our most important decisions."

"Yes, it definitely is, but we won't have time to cover that in today's meeting," Super Retirement Planner agreed.

"In a future meeting, we will do an analysis of your benefits. Although we want to get a lot out of your Social Security benefits, what we really want to do is to *optimize* your Social Security benefits. That means we need them to fit into your overall retirement income plan. So we'll start out by designing the blueprint for your nest egg and then we'll see how your Social Security benefits can best support that. Does that make sense?"

"Absolutely," Jill responded.

"Okay, great," replied Super Retirement Planner. "That should be your list of assets. Let's move on to the next step."

HOW MUCH INCOME DO YOU NEED?

"The next step is to determine how much income you will need in retirement. Have you talked about that or given it any thought?"

Jack began flipping through his notebook until he found the page he was seeking.

"The truth is that when this whole process started, we didn't have a clue what income we would need! But as we've gone through this, Jill and I have sat down and tried to figure it out. We liked the idea of sorting it into two categories: essential and nonessential."

Super Retirement Planner nodded in understanding. "That's a great way of doing it. Many of our clients just come up with an overall spending number, but some of our clients like separating their spending into those two categories. So what did you all come up with for your different categories of expenses?"

Jack looked over his notes.

"We came up with $5,500 a month of essential expenses, and we would like to see if we can add another $1,500 a month for non-essential expenses. I have to say, I was surprised at how big those numbers are. Would you say these are normal or acceptable?"

Super Retirement Planner smiled.

"Jack, I get that question all the time. We have a huge range of spending between all of our clients, and it varies for all kinds of reasons. I wouldn't worry about how it compares to anyone else. The most important thing is for us to figure out if your resources can support that level of income."

"Now let's total up your Social Security benefits at full retirement and any pensions you have. How much does that add up to per month?"

Jack reviewed the numbers on his notepad. "It would be right around $4,000 per month."

INCOME FOR YOUR ESSENTIAL EXPENSES

"Great," replied Super Retirement Planner. "So your essential expenses are $5,500 a month, and you will have $4,000 per month of income. So your GRIP is 73 percent, which is good.

That means we need to create $1,500 a month of income from your nest egg. We believe that when dealing with your essential expenses, that risk of principal needs to be avoided. Therefore, that $1,500 a month needs to be created by allocating to the Foundation.

"Now, there are a lot of different ways we could do that. But to keep things simple, let's assume we simply shop for an annuity that will generate guaranteed lifetime income of $1,500 a month. We will look for a highly rated annuity company that will give you the best payout. Essentially, what we will be trying to figure out is what is the least amount of money we can put into an annuity to generate $1,500 per month guaranteed as long as both of you or even one of you is still living. Does that make sense?"

"It does," Jack replied. "I know we've both heard all kinds of things about annuities, and you said we need to be agnostic about which solutions we use. But I think we will just want to make sure we understand how they work. Also, can you give us an idea of how much that would need to be used to create that income?"

"Yes, once again, you have it exactly right, Jack," Super Retirement Planner said with an empathetic nod.

"It's important to be agnostic as to what options we end up using. But at the same time, we want you to understand those options. Today, we are discussing these options only at a high level. In one of our future meetings, we will dig into the details so you can see the pros and cons of each option.

"Regarding the amount, I would estimate that at your age, to generate $1,500 a month guaranteed, we would need to allocate around $375,000. So that would be the first allocation of your blueprint: at least $375,000 to the Foundation."

Jack and Jill looked at each other and smiled.

"All right! It feels good to finally get this started!" Jack said.

"By the way, I think this is a good time to mention something that I've learned over the years," Super Retirement Planner added. "As we design your blueprint, please remember that nothing you decide to do with your money will please everyone. That means if you're discussing this with family or friends, plenty of people will tell you that something you did was foolish or crazy.

"For those situations, I have a favorite quote. It is from Dr. David Babble, who is the Professor Emeritus at the esteemed Wharton School of Finance. When asked about people disagreeing with his use of annuities for his own retirement, he replied,

'Let them criticize; let us sleep.'"

Jack laughed. "I love that!"

Super Retirement Planner continued, "Okay, then, now we have your essential expenses covered and need to move on to your nonessential expenses. This is the first time that we can consider your risk tolerance. Someone who is extremely conservative may wish to cover their nonessential expenses with Foundation accounts as well. But someone who is more moderate or aggressive can seek to use Walls investments to generate income."

WHAT IS YOUR RISK TOLERANCE?

"Let me ask both of you individually when it comes to your investments, based on where you are in life today, to rate yourselves on a scale of one to ten. Think of one being someone who is really aggressive and isn't worried when the stock market crashes. On the other hand, a ten is someone who doesn't care at all about returns and is content to have all their money in savings accounts. Jill, let's start with you. Where would you put yourself from one to ten?"

Jill was a little startled. She felt like she had just been put on the spot.

Super Retirement Planner saw the concern in her eyes and added, "Jill, please don't worry. There are no right or wrong answers. Just take a moment and answer honestly."

Jill composed herself before answering.

"Well, I know for a fact that I'm not a one because the stock market does worry me. On the other hand, I would definitely like to get more than the return of a savings account. I guess since we're so close to retirement, safety is more important to me than trying to get a really high return. So I think I will rate myself a seven."

"Very good." Super Retirement Planner smiled.

He knew that a lot of people struggled with this exercise, but he could tell that Jill had considered it carefully. Although there is no perfect way to label anyone's risk tolerance, he believed that she had most likely rated herself accurately or very close to it.

"All right, Jack, how about you?"

Jack looked over to Jill and smiled.

"I was definitely more aggressive when I was younger. I think before 2008, I would have been somewhere around two or three. But like Jill said, I have to consider where we are in life, and we know that we can't afford to lose a large part of what we've worked so hard for. I'm going to rate myself as a six. I think that safety is more important than returns, but I also hope that we've got a lot more life ahead of us, and I want to do everything I can to make sure we never run out of money."

"Excellent," Super Retirement Planner replied.

Sometimes this particular exercise went very smoothly, but sometimes it was a challenge. He felt like Jack and Jill had done great, so he decided to test them one last time.

"Let me ask one more question. Do each of you think that the other rated themselves properly?"

Jack and Jill looked at each other and chuckled.

"Yes, I do," Jack replied. "I think that before 2008, Jill was probably quite a bit more conservative than me. But after that crash and now that we're learning so much about retirement planning, I think we are quite close to each other. We both would like some returns but understand that safety is a bigger priority."

Jill agreed, "Yes, Jack was definitely much more aggressive years ago, but he has done a really good job of getting more conservative as we have gotten closer to retirement."

Super Retirement Planner had a big smile on his face.

"That's awesome. I commend you both for a few things. First, you both understand that you should not and cannot invest the same way in your sixties as you did in your thirties. Second, scores around six and seven are right in the range that allows us to allocate your funds in a way to meet your goals. For example, if you both said you were a ten, that is a challenge because that means you both want all your money to be placed in the Foundation.

"On the other hand, if you both said a one, that tells me that you probably don't understand where you are in life right now and how critical it is to lower risk heading into retirement.

"And finally, I hope you both realize what a blessing it is that your scores are so close together. I've met with couples who have scores that are really far apart. Imagine if you were married and one of you was a three and the other was a nine. It may sound silly, but that kind of difference can be at the root of a lot of marital stress because it's difficult to design a blueprint in a way that works for both people."

"Wow, I had never thought of it that way," Jack said. "I guess we are fortunate."

"I'll be honest," Jill added. "When we were younger and Jack was more aggressive with our money, I wasn't comfortable with it. But like I said, I sincerely appreciate how you've changed over the years. Now I feel like we are on the same page and ready to accomplish our goals together!"

Jack smiled and held Jill's hand in his.

"That's why we're here right now," he said.

Jill smiled back.

Super Retirement Planner was smiling, too.

"Jill, thank you for sharing that. It's always great to see a couple working together."

INCOME FOR YOUR NONESSENTIAL EXPENSES

"Now let's go back to discussing your income and expenses. We already tackled your essential expenses and need to decide how to plan for your $1,500 a month of nonessential expenses. Since you have rated yourselves in the six to seven range of risk tolerance, that tells me that we can incorporate all three levels in your blueprint. For someone who is retired or close to it like you are, we like to use dividends from Walls investments to generate income for nonessential expenses.

"Once again, without getting into all the details and looking from a high level, let's assume the Walls investments are generating dividends at a rate of 5 percent per year. So to generate $1,500 a month, that works out to $18,000 of dividends per year. That means we would need to allocate $360,000 toward the Walls.

"In our next meeting, we'll discuss further what exactly this would look like, but I'm sure Endowment Edward explained that it would be a mixture of income-producing investments designed to provide as much diversification as possible. Does that make sense?"

Jack and Jill looked at each other and nodded in agreement.

"All right, so that's $375,000 so far in the Foundation and

$360,000 in the Walls," Jack added. "That's about half of our savings and investments. We're making good progress!"

ADDING IN THE ROOF

"Absolutely," Super Retirement Planner agreed. "Now that we've covered your essential and non-essential income needs, we like to consider the Roof for the first time.

"Generally, we recommend allocating to the Roof as long as your risk tolerance score isn't something like a nine or a ten. Since you are in the six to seven range, I don't think we would want a huge amount in the Roof, but we definitely want something there for all the reasons that Wall Street William described.

"As a starting point, we look to Benjamin Graham. He is considered Warren Buffett's teacher and by many as one of the greatest investing minds in US history.

"He believed that even the most conservative investor should have at least 25 percent of their money in the stock market at all times.[29] So as a starting point, I would suggest we next allocate 25 percent, or $375,000, to the Roof. Although I don't want to get into the nitty-gritty details of allocations in today's discussion, I do want to quickly address another concept that we believe is fundamental to our Roof allocation decisions."

DYNAMIC REBALANCING

"Dynamic rebalancing essentially refers to considering various

---

29 Myers, Daniel. "Benjamin Graham's 3 Most Timeless Investment Principles." *Investopedia*, Investopedia, 28 Aug. 2020, https://www.investopedia.com/articles/basics/07/grahamprinciples.asp.

factors of where the markets and economy currently stand and how it relates to your allocation. On the one hand, this should be obvious because we all have the goal of buying low and selling high whenever possible. On the other hand, we also know that predicting the markets or the economy is impossible. So you might be wondering why I would even bring this up."

Jack leaned forward. "We know it's impossible to predict the future, but we still want you to be able to!"

They all shared a good laugh.

"Rather than trying to predict the future, what we're referring to here is doing whatever we can to put the odds on your side," Super Retirement Planner continued.

"Let's consider the US stock market. As we're sitting here today, it has lasted more than ten years on an upswing. That is the longest stretch in our country's recorded history, which goes all the way back to the 1800s! That information alone makes many people, myself included, fearful of when and how big the next stock market drop will be."

"You're definitely not the only one!" Jack added.

Super Retirement Planner wasn't surprised as so many of his clients had voiced similar concerns.

"Absolutely. In addition to how much time this up-market has lasted, we like to look at other measures that attempt to track whether the stock market is undervalued, overvalued, or appropriately valued. One highly respected measure is the Shiller

CAPE ratio. In simple terms, this attempts to measure the stock market's value versus how profitable the stocks are.

"The idea is simply, if the stocks that make up the market are similarly profitable to how they've been in the past, are they valued higher, lower, or the same as they have been historically? If they're undervalued, that should be a good indicator that an investment would potentially be 'buying low.'

"On the other hand, if the stock market is overvalued, then we would be 'buying high,' which is certainly not what we want to do!

"Let's take a look at a chart of the Shiller CAPE ratio going back to the late 1880s."[30]

"If you're like me, some things immediately jump out to you when you look at the chart. The first thing is that there are only a few spikes where this measure has gone much higher than the rest of the periods. Those dates were September 1929, July 1999, and May 2007.

---

30 *Shiller PE Ratio*, https://www.multpl.com/shiller-pe.

"Each of those peaks was followed by a major stock market crash within a year."

"Yes, 2008 was such a scary time," Jill agreed. "There were times we received our statements in the mail and were too scared to open them."

"You definitely weren't alone," Super Retirement Planner replied. "This was another market drop that instilled in me the belief that we cannot just tell people to put money in the stock market and to ride out all its downturns. Retirement is too important to just hope it will work out.

"That brings me to today. Over the last few years, this measure has been floating at one of the highest levels ever. What does that tell both of you about the stock market right now?"

Jack and Jill looked at each other before Jack tentatively replied, "Well, it definitely seems too high."

Super Retirement Planner nodded. "Yes, I agree. So the good news is that we know that the US stock market appears overpriced. The bad news is that this measure cannot predict *when* the markets will adjust. As I mentioned, this measure has been high for a few years now. So we believe that even though it cannot predict the future, it can tell us when we should be taking less risk.

"Therefore, we still believe the Roof has its place in your allocation, but we recommend that we make use of the strategies to try to reduce downside risk that Wall Street William outlined in your meeting with him. Again, we'll dig more into the details in our next meeting."

FINALIZING YOUR ALLOCATIONS

"I think we understand the value of having something in the Roof, and I also think we definitely like the idea of trying to reduce the risk on those investments," Jack replied.

"But I do have a question: we've now covered the Foundation, Walls, and Roof, but by my math, you've allocated only $1.11 million of our $1.5 million of savings and investments. What the heck do we do with the rest of it?"

"That is a terrific question, Jack," Super Retirement Planner said with a smile. "It's actually good news that we haven't allocated everything already. Remember, we started by making sure we had enough in the right areas to create the income you will need at retirement. If those allocations accounted for more than 100 percent of your nest egg, that means we have real problems. But in your case, we have some flexibility.

"The first suggestion I would make is that 25 percent in the Foundation is too low for a couple who is close to retirement and with your risk tolerance. So right away, I would suggest we increase that to a total of at least 40 percent, which means another $225,000. These funds could be used for some combination of attempting to get a decent return while maintaining the safety of principal as well as structuring something to boost your income later in retirement to protect you from inflation. Does that make sense?"

"Absolutely," Jill said. "I'm all on board with protecting us from Lady Longevity and the Invisible Enemy."

"Perfect," Super Retirement Planner responded. "Finally, that leaves a remaining 8 percent of your nest egg to allocate. Based on where we are with current allocations and markets, I would suggest we add this to the Walls. Simply put, we want to avoid adding to the Roof until we see more normal pricing in the markets."

He then presented them with the breakdown they had determined:

- Foundation: $600,000 or 40 percent
- Walls: $525,000 or 35 percent
- Roof: $375,000 or 25 percent

Super Retirement Planner paused to let his summary sink in.

"How does that feel?"

Jack and Jill stared at the page that Super Retirement Planner was using and then looked at each other. Jack responded first.

"I definitely want to hear how Jill feels, but it feels amazing to me. This feels kind of like the finish line of running a marathon. When we started, we didn't have a clue how to retire off our nest egg. Now I can see a clear plan of how we can design our blueprint to give us the best chance to accomplish our goals.

"Jill, I'm really curious to hear what you think."

Jill smiled at Jack.

"I'm so happy to say that I feel exactly the same way you do," she added. "I was nervous about how to retire, like you said. And I was nervous about what we were supposed to do with our money and about things like trusting all our money in the stock market. This approach just seems like it makes so much sense."

WHAT'S THE DOWNSIDE?

"Super Retirement Planner, hopefully, you don't mind me asking this," Jack added. "You taught us that there are always one or more downsides to every investment. So is that the case when designing a blueprint with the Foundation, Walls, and Roof? What are the downsides we should consider?"

Super Retirement Planner smiled.

"Jack, that is a great point. When you're dealing with your money, it's always good to consider what the downsides are. I think of it this way: the downsides are simply the opposite of what we've created.

"The goal of what we've built for you is to provide you with income, both guaranteed and based on dividends, potential for growth from the Roof, inflation protection through the Walls, liquidity for emergencies, and diversification for when the economy and/or the markets are down. We're essentially attempting to give you a little bit of everything. That means that you aren't getting all of anything, right?

"The downside is that depending on the circumstances, less diversified approaches will sometimes do better than your allocation. Even if we picked the 'perfect' allocation for you, there will be years when the stock market soars. You'll hear about it in the news, your friends will be talking about it, and human nature will dictate that you are disappointed, frustrated, or even unhappy with your allocation. And this may happen often! Yet, you still have the right allocation."

"I think we understand," Jill added. "The stock market is just front and center in the news. Anytime it's down, we're going to feel really smart because of our allocation. Anytime it's up, we have to remember all the reasons we diversified so we don't get caught up in 'missing out.'"

"Great points, honey," Jack chimed in. "I will admit that maybe this is a silver lining to the crash in 2008. Maybe without it, I would feel greedy when the stock market goes up. Since we lost so much money in 2008, I think it will help me remember that it would be flat-out crazy for us to have all of our money at risk like that."

"Awesome," Super Retirement Planner said in appreciation of both of their responses.

"That perspective can help both of you truly enjoy your retirement instead of constantly worrying and stressing about your nest egg.

"I'll add that although the stock market will most likely be the most common culprit, it's not the only one. Let's say that out of nowhere, there was massive inflation in the United States. In that case, the Walls investments may perform much better than your other allocations. Or let's say that the entire economy comes crashing down without warning. In that case, the Foundation accounts could easily do far better than the others.

"To summarize, the downside to this approach is that you are admitting two things: that there are no perfect investments and you cannot predict the future. Therefore, you are willing to divvy your money up into different types of accounts, but this downside is actually quite freeing. By realizing you cannot predict the future, it frees you to spread your money out so that you don't have to worry about what comes next. Instead, you can focus on the things that are truly important in life."

"That sounds priceless," Jack said, smiling at Jill.

"I couldn't agree more," Super Retirement Planner concurred. "Before you go today, can I quickly give you a broader view of a comprehensive retirement plan and how the blueprint for your nest egg fits into it?"

Jack leaned forward. "Let's do it!"

SUMMARY OF MAJOR POINTS

Three principles of designing your blueprint:

- Focus on your goals.
- Take an agnostic view.
- It must be custom-built.
  - Which investing phase are you in?
  - What is your GRIP?
  - Match your allocation with your comfort with risk.
  - Allow for personal preferences.
- How to build your blueprint:
  - Lay out all your materials (resources).
  - How much income do you need?
  - Determine income from Foundation and Walls
  - Add the Roof.
  - Finalize your allocations.
- Dynamic rebalancing considers where the markets stand when making your allocations.
- Remember that your diversified allocation won't "win" all of the time.

Chapter 10

═══

JUST ONE PIECE... OR PEACE?

Super Retirement Planner continued right into his summary.

"As you both know, we believe that this approach can be the secret to successfully handling your nest egg through retirement. We also believe that this investment plan is only one of the five plans that you must have in place to truly have a comprehensive retirement plan.

"Let's quickly take a look at these areas."

INVESTMENT PLAN

"I think it's safe to say that we've already covered how to build your investment plan in tremendous detail. That leads us into a second area of your retirement plan."

INCOME PLAN

"Although we haven't fully formed an income plan for you, we've definitely discussed some of the basics. The following are must-haves for all retirees plus one just for married couples." He listed:

- Consistent and reliable income
- Income that protects your lifestyle from the effects of inflation
- Income that lasts a lifetime (or two!)
- For married couples: income that continues if one of you passes away

"If a married couple hasn't considered all four of these items, then they do not have a comprehensive retirement income plan. Simply put, having a plan for all four of these areas should give anyone a tremendous amount of confidence and peace of mind.

"We've talked about your Social Security, Jill's state pension, and how we will generate income from the Foundation and Walls. But that is not a comprehensive income plan. In future meetings, we will talk further about how to make the most of your Social Security benefits, what options you might have with your state pension, projections of inflation throughout your retirement, how your income would be affected if one of you passed away, and finally, long-term projections to try to make sure you never run out of money.

"I'm sure you can tell that there is still a lot of work to be done to complete this part of your plan!"

Jack looked over at Jill. "Okay, I'm definitely glad I'm not the one who has to figure all of that out!"

Jill smiled and rubbed Jack's arm.

Super Retirement Planner smiled and continued. "Very good! Let's look at the next area."

TAX PLAN

"Closely related to the income plan is your tax plan," he said. "Comprehensive retirement planning includes a strategy to examine your tax liabilities, with the hope of decreasing your tax bill whenever possible.

"Our goal is to ensure that you are never paying unnecessary taxes and giving you the peace of mind knowing that you are being as tax-smart as possible.

"For most people planning for retirement, a few of the most common areas of tax planning are:

ANALYZE YOUR NEST EGG'S TAX CONSEQUENCES

"We can categorize your money into one of three tax buckets," Super Retirement Planner said, then defined the buckets.

1. **Taxable:** This would include any taxable accounts such as bank accounts and investment accounts that you receive a tax bill on annually.
2. **Tax-deferred:** This would include many accounts that are designed for retirement: 401(k)s, traditional IRAs, 403bs, and 457s. These are powerful for helping you grow your money. However, eventually, those taxes need to be paid, either by you or by your family.
3. **Tax-free:** The most well-known tax-free options are the Roth IRA and Roth 401(k). There are other options as well. But basically, these accounts are designed for tax-free withdrawals.

"The first step is to determine what you currently have. The next step is to see what the tax consequences of those accounts are.

"Finally, this part of your plan will help you analyze your options to see if changes could help you lower your income taxes either now or in the future.

"I can tell you, this area of planning has been one of the most exciting for us in the last few years. Just by making smart decisions related to these three tax 'buckets,' we have clients who expect to have literally hundreds of thousands of dollars more either in income throughout their retirement or in larger nest eggs for them or their heirs."

This definitely caught Jack's attention.

"That sounds amazing," he exclaimed. "I hope we can look at that soon!"

Super Retirement Planner chuckled. "Yes, it's definitely on the list!"

PLAN TO TRY TO AVOID A HIGHER TAX BRACKET

"With today's tax rates, there is a federal tax rate jump from 12 to 22 percent. If by planning you can keep yourself in the 12 percent federal tax bracket, hopefully, it is clear to see that could mean a huge tax savings to you."

"If you can help us never pay more than 12 percent federal taxes, that might be the most exciting thing I've heard!" Jack interjected.

"Well, I don't know if that's possible," Super Retirement Planner said with a smile, "but I promise you that our goal is to keep your taxes as low as possible!"

PLAN TAXES IN CASE ONE OF YOU PASSES AWAY

"Tax rules change dramatically if one of you or both of you pass away. So we want to do an analysis ahead of time to make sure neither of you nor your loved ones has any unpleasant surprises from the IRS."

HEALTHCARE AND INSURANCE PLAN

"The next area is your healthcare and insurance plan. A great retirement game plan includes not only offense but defense as well. Your healthcare and insurance plan should address the possible answers to some major questions that are still unknown." He posed the questions:

- How can we protect you from a major financial drain for medical care?
- What if one or both of you experience a nursing care need?
- What could happen to you financially if you or a loved one passes away?

"This is even more important than most realize. According to the Employee Benefit Research Institute, a sixty-five-year-old couple with typical prescription-drug expenses will need $295,000 to enjoy a 75 percent chance of being able to pay all their remaining lifetime medical bills, and $360,000 to have a 90 percent chance.[31]

---

31 Employee Benefit Research Institute, October 2015, https://www.ebri.org/pdf/notespdf/ ebri_notes_10_oct15_ hlthsvgs_db-dc.pdf.

"Our goal is to help you plan to make the best use of your available resources to provide an appropriate level of protection for you throughout your retirement. This includes reviewing such things as health insurance, Medicare, long-term care and insurance options, and life insurance."

"Yes, the unknown of medical costs has always been a worry of mine," Jill said. "And I had no idea it could be that bad."

"You're right," Super Retirement Planner replied in a soothing tone.

"It can't be predicted, but having a plan for medical costs is the first and most important step."

ESTATE PLAN

"The best estate plan will allow you to leave the remainder of your unused wealth to your beneficiaries with minimal taxes, cost, and delays. We want you to know that when you pass on, those you have designated to inherit something will receive the most possible and in accordance with your wishes. This requires a discussion and review of legal and beneficiary documents.

"As a married couple, even more important is a plan in case one of you passes away before the other. In addition to being one of the most difficult times of your life emotionally, it can have enormous effects on you financially." Super Retirement Planner mentioned a few examples of financial changes that can happen when a spouse passes away:

- Adjustments to your Social Security income
- Adjustments or elimination of pension income

- Adjustments or elimination of annuity income
- Decisions to be made related to investments that mature upon death
- Tax-related decisions on investment accounts
- Retitling of joint accounts and those owned by the deceased
- Claiming of life insurance benefits

"A comprehensive plan must be prepared for this, and having a planning team working with you should give you great comfort that you won't be on your own if this happens."

"This is a great example of why handling your own investments just doesn't make any sense to me," Jill jumped in while looking at Jack. "I think I'm a reasonably intelligent person. But Jack, if you passed away, I would be clueless about how that affects our finances and what I would need to do with our money."

Jack grabbed Jill's hand and responded, "First of all, you *are* very intelligent! But as we've learned how complicated all this is, I do much better understand why this process would be valuable to you if something happened to me. And hopefully, we'll both be around for a long time, so we'll both benefit from all this planning."

"That sounds good to me!" Jill said with a loving smile.

Super Retirement Planner returned their smiles. "You just summed up the point: prepare for the worst and hope for the best. We hope you're both around a really long time to enjoy all that you've worked for. But if something happens to you, all the planning will be in place."

THE DA VINCI BRIDGE

"As valuable as all five of these plans are, it is just as important that all of them work together. Your investment plan must support your income plan and your income plan must work with your tax plan. In addition, strong healthcare, insurance, and estate plans can protect the rest of your plans. The most powerful example of this that I have found is called the Da Vinci bridge. One of the lesser-known inventions of famous inventor Leonardo Da Vinci was a self-supporting bridge."

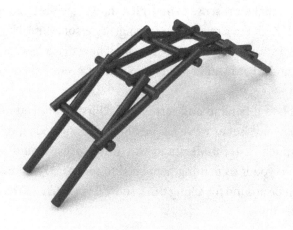

"In 1502, government leaders sought ideas and proposals for a bridge that would connect Istanbul to its neighbor city Galata. Da Vinci submitted his proposal, which used its own weight to support itself.[32] This is a perfect example of a well-constructed retirement plan.

32   David L. Chandler | MIT News Office. "Engineers Put Leonardo Da Vinci's Bridge Design to the Test." *MIT News | Massachusetts Institute of Technology*, news. http://news.mit.edu/2019/leonardo-da-vinci-bridge-test-1010.

"You see, it's so common for us to focus on one individual area of our retirement planning. Some people focus exclusively on what the stock market is doing. Others pay all their attention to the next election in fear of what it will do to their investments. Or perhaps you check on your 401(k) balance every day, tinkering with the investment options.

"Of course, all of those examples are related to an investment plan. Other examples might be a focus on when to claim Social Security. Or perhaps someone has a good pension from their employer and is completely dependent on it. Or think of someone who is dealing with a sick parent and they lie awake at night worrying about how they would ever be able to pay for long-term care expenses for themselves?

"The reality is that whatever this one thing is, it is focused on because it is either the 'thing' that you are most comfortable with, or it is the 'thing' you are most worried about.

"But one 'thing' cannot create a successful retirement. It reminds me of back in 2005 when Staples introduced the Easy Button. Do you both remember that?"

Jack and Jill chuckled at the memory.

"Oh, yes," Jack responded. "They advertised that during football games all the time. Have a problem? Press the button, and it's solved! 'That was easy!'"

"Exactly," Super Retirement Planner responded. "Now, wouldn't it be nice if we had an Easy Button for our retirement? But I'm sure you realize with all you've been through, that just isn't possible. Retirement is too complicated and way too important to just sit around and hope that an Easy Button will magically appear.

"You must have all five areas of your retirement plan. Each of those areas will be built with different pieces, and all of these pieces need to not only fit together but also have to be able to support each other.

"And that is why the Da Vinci bridge is such a powerful analogy. Take a look again at what it looks like. Our goal is to build you a retirement plan that works the same way. Does that make sense?"

"Yes, that's such a helpful visual," Jack replied. "I had never heard of the Da Vinci bridge before, and it is really quite amazing that it can support itself, *and* it is a cool reminder that the different parts of our retirement plan need to do the same."

THE SYMPHONY

"Perfect," Super Retirement Planner replied. "Because this is so important, I'll share one more analogy before we finish. Have you all ever been to the symphony?"

Jill's eyes lit up. "Oh, yes! Only a couple of times, but we loved it!"

"Tell me, did you get there before they started?" Super Retirement Planner asked. "And if so, what do you remember?"

Jill paused, then said, "Well, before they get started, everyone is on stage warming up."

Super Retirement Planner nodded. "That's right, everyone is

warming up—all at the same time. Now, what does that sound like?"

"Oh, it's a mess!" Jill recalled with a laugh. "It sounds like cats fighting!"

"You've got it," Super Retirement Planner said. "You have all different members of the symphony playing different instruments, and they're all playing different notes and different times. None of them are paying any attention to anything but themselves and making sure their notes sound right.

"But then the conductor walks from offstage and approaches the little podium. As this happens, all the noise gets quieter and quieter. The moment that the conductor stands up on that little podium and taps the baton on the music stand, it is completely silent, and all eyes are on him or her.

"This is a perfect example of what we do. Over the course of the last forty years or so, you have accumulated so many different instruments related to your retirement. Think of all of the things that you might have." He gave them some ideas:

- Your current income and tax withholdings
- Your home
- 401(k)
- Checking and savings accounts
- Certificates of deposit
- Stocks or mutual funds
- Roth IRAs
- Life insurance policies
- Health insurance
- Access to Medicare

- Disability insurance
- Homeowners insurance
- Social Security benefits
- Pension benefits

"It goes on and on," he explained. "Now think for a second about what all of these have in common. They all came into your lives apart from everything else on the list. If you're like most people, you've accumulated this list of resources, and none of them work together. It's like the warm-up before the symphony.

"Well, now you're here, and now the symphony is about to begin. Because we are the conductors. We are here to coordinate all the various resources you have and make them work together. Ultimately, the goal will be that you can simply sit back, relax, and enjoy the music."

"I bet that Jill agrees that we are ready to enjoy the music!" Jack said.

"Absolutely," Jill agreed. "I love both analogies. Let's make sure our bridge is self-supporting, and let's make sure our symphony makes beautiful music!"

Super Retirement Planner smiled. "That's what we love to do, and we're excited to do it for you as well!"

SUMMARY OF MAJOR POINTS

A comprehensive retirement plan includes planning in five areas:

INVESTMENT PLAN

- Custom-build your blueprint

INCOME PLAN

- Consistent and reliable income
- Income that protects your lifestyle from inflation
- Income that lasts a lifetime (or two!)
- Income that continues if one of you passes away

TAX PLAN

- Analyze your nest egg's tax consequences
- Plan to avoid going into a higher tax bracket
- Tax planning in case you pass away

HEALTHCARE AND INSURANCE PLAN

- Protection from medical care financial drain
- Plan for nursing care, if needed
- Financial plan if you pass away

ESTATE PLAN

- Bequeath with minimal taxes, expenses, and delays
- Plan if one spouse predeceases the other

Each area of your plan supports each other—just like the pieces of the Da Vinci bridge.

The different pieces of your comprehensive retirement plan fit together to create beautiful music!

EPILOGUE

I hope you've enjoyed joining Jack and Jill on their journey. Oh, are you wondering what happened to them? Why, they retired happily ever after, of course!

But what about you? Do you have your very own Super Retirement Planner? One of the greatest challenges of dealing with your finances is finding the right person and team to help you. That's why we've developed the following ten steps to help you find the right fit for you.

STEP 1: DON'T GO IT ALONE!

I am sure if you've made it this far, you know that we believe in the value of having a team working with you. The rules of the game are always changing. You need trusted guides who focus on solving these special types of financial problems. These trusted guides won't be found in the form of your favorite bank teller, nor at the local coffee shop or beauty shop. The greatest protection available will be with specialized teams of professionals who will help you build and manage the plans that were covered in this book.

STEP 2: BEWARE OF A "PLANNER" WHO WILL HELP YOU IMPLEMENT INVESTMENTS IF NO PLAN IS PREPARED.

Buying financial products without a plan is like having surgery without an exam. A doctor who performs surgery without an exam would be malpractice!

The same holds true for a financial advisor who sells a product without an analysis. If you take away the planning process, you are left with nothing more than a product salesperson.

Now, a plan may be many things. It can be a short one-pager all the way up to a thick set of charts and graphs. Even if the written plan is short, the interview process must not be.

The best planning is not due to the thickness of the plan but because of the depth of the interview. The planner must ask about all your issues, not just the ones they can make money on. For example, they should ask about your taxes, home financing, company benefits, insurance, estate planning, retirement goals, investments, and so forth.

A good advisor knows how to get to know you, your goals, and your fears. If you feel they truly understand your emotions as well as your finances, then you may be with the right advisor!

STEP 3: IF THE PLANNER CHARGES A PLANNING FEE, ASK HOW MUCH OF THE FEE MUST BE PAID IN ADVANCE AND IF THEY COVER A SPECIFIC AMOUNT OF TIME, SUCH AS TWELVE MONTHS, OR IF THEY COVER THE COMPLETION AND IMPLEMENTATION OF YOUR PLAN.

In my opinion, you are usually better off working with an advisor who charges their planning fees on a flat basis, no matter how many hours they spend with you or on your planning. Hourly charges can work, but I have seen many instances where disputes have arisen because of the number of hours being billed. I have also seen many cases where people felt there are too many hours being charged, then stop the planning process because they feel it's running too much money—thus prohibiting them from getting their planning finished.

STEP 4: ASK THE PLANNER IF THEY CHARGE FEES FOR MANAGING SOME OR ALL OF YOUR MONEY INSTEAD OF OR IN ADDITION TO PLANNING FEES AND PRODUCT SALES COMMISSIONS.

Some financial advisors charge for money management (sometimes called asset management) services in various ways, almost always based on a percentage of the money they are managing for you. These fees can range from 1 to 3 percent per year in most cases (including investment costs). So the more money they are managing, the more the fees you'll pay.

This method of charging money management fees is not necessarily bad, but you should know how much the fees are, how they are billed, and what kind of discounts are available for larger accounts. Even though this is a structure that can work, it is a lot more appealing for someone starting out investing as opposed to someone near or in retirement. You can quickly do the math on how much 1 to 3 percent of hundreds of thousands or millions of dollars is—every year!

Be sure to get clarification as to whether these money management fees are separate from financial planning fees. Some advisors will charge financial planning fees and then charge additional money management fees on top of the planning fees. With this type of advisor, make sure to ask them if you pay them for planning fees, if you will be required to use their money management services, or if you're free to invest your money based on their advice with any money manager you choose.

Some advisors will not charge you a planning fee and just charge the money management fees if you let them manage the money. You should ask if they do any kind of financial planning *before* making money management recommendations. If they say they don't or give you some sales pitch instead of a plan, get out of there quickly! (Remember step 3.)

Another method to watch out for is if the advisor charges a money management fee *in addition to* product sales commissions. If you are expected to pay 1 to 3 percent of your money for management as well as paying fees for such things as mutual funds and variable annuities, your investment fees will almost certainly get expensive. Make sure you're clear on how this works.

One point I will add: I've had many people over the years tell me that they are uncomfortable asking a financial professional how they are compensated. I completely understand that this can be awkward. However, please understand a few things. First of all, the reason you need to ask isn't your fault, and it isn't their fault either. It's the system. Financial professionals can structure their fees in so many different ways, and many of them are difficult to understand and essentially invisible. Asking is the only way for you to know.

This is important. This is your money you're dealing with. It's also your retirement. You get only one chance to get it right.

Finally, if the financial professional is uncomfortable talking about how they are compensated or if they are offended at all, that is another huge red flag. You know darn well that no financial professional works for free, so why would they be uncomfortable talking about it? And if the question is brushed off, in my opinion, that is enough reason to look elsewhere.

STEP 5: IF THE PLANNER CHARGES FEES, ASK IF THEY PROVIDE YOU WITH A WRITTEN, 100 PERCENT GUARANTEE OF UNCONDITIONAL SATISFACTION.

If they are so sure they can help you, they should back up that promise with an ironclad guarantee. The benefits you receive must exceed the cost of the planning/advice. You are the only person who can determine the amount of help you have received, and the benefit received cannot be determined until the plan has been completed and presented to you. There should be no question in your mind that you have received more benefit than cost. If not, then the fee should be adjusted or returned.

(FYI: They **cannot** guarantee anything about any investments you decide to make through them. It is against the law for them to do so unless the product has written guarantees built into it.)

STEP 6: IF THE FINANCIAL PROFESSIONAL DOESN'T CHARGE FEES, MAKE SURE YOU HAVE A CLEAR UNDERSTANDING OF HOW THEY ARE COMPENSATED.

Generally, if they don't charge a planning fee and they don't charge an asset management fee, they are likely being compensated by commission. Although our industry often considers "commission" to be like a four-letter word, this type of professional isn't necessarily bad. However, it is critical that you can reach a point in your relationship of trust. The last position you want to be in is questioning whether something is being recommended because it's the best thing for you or if it is being recommended because it pays a nice commission. This distinction is critical. It is the difference between finding your trusted advisor or dealing with a financial salesperson.

Take car shopping as an example. If I go to a Ford dealership, I know the salespeople there are going to try to sell me a Ford. They aren't trying to convince me that they are unbiased. They may help me figure out which Ford is the best car for me, but they aren't going to recommend that I head over to a Toyota dealership.

There's nothing wrong with salespeople. The problem is when someone holds themselves out as someone whom you should trust—especially for something as important as your finances. I know what I'm getting when I talk to a Ford salesperson. You need to figure out what you're getting when you deal with a financial professional who works by commission only.

STEP 7: BEWARE OF FINANCIAL ADVISOR "EMPLOYEES."

If the advisor works *for* a brokerage house (Merrill Lynch, Smith Barney, Morgan Stanley, Wells Fargo Securities, etc.) or *for* an insurance company (John Hancock, MetLife, Northwestern Mutual, etc.), you want to be careful. They may still be the right person. However, you need to realize that these advisors almost always have limitations on what they can and cannot do. These limitations are dictated by their home office. And how much does their home office know about you?

As a result, while a particular planning strategy may be particularly valuable for you and your unique circumstances, an advisor with one of these organizations may not be able to help you due to home office-driven limitations. And even if they can help you, their home office may not allow them (for various reasons that have nothing to do with you) to use the optimal financial vehicles for that strategy. So be careful when dealing with someone who is not independent.

STEP 8: BEWARE OF ONLINE "RESOURCES."

Information online should be viewed with a very skeptical eye. Today, it is not uncommon for retirees and their children to get online to do research. The critical questions should be, are you getting information from a credible source? This can be very difficult to decipher online.

An additional problem is information overload. If you research the keywords "when should I claim Social Security" on Google today, you will find over 688 million articles, websites, and "resources" to review.

The problem is, before you finish your review of these 688 million resources, you could be dead without having followed through on any of the advice. Obviously, this would defeat your original planning goals. Now, you must do your due diligence and research, but be sure you're researching the right thing—getting the right help. Remember step 1 (Don't go it alone).

Finally, remember the first lesson in chapter 5: there is no such thing as an unbiased financial professional. Well, the same goes for online advice. Anytime you see an absolute statement, it is due to a bias. Using common sense, do you think all of the following statements are really true?

- **No one** should ever place money into annuities.
- **Everyone** should defer their Social Security until age seventy.
- The **only** type of life insurance **anyone** should own is term insurance.
- The stock market **always** beats other investments.

Of course, it would be impossible for anyone to prove such statements. Yet comments like these abound. Online information can be helpful, but don't forget about the bias of the author.

STEP 9: DEMAND PROOF!

There is nothing worse than getting sold a bad idea. Slick talk can be very persuasive, but in the end, it may prove financially disastrous. When seeking professional advice, we recommend that you ask the following to ensure that you are being advised by an accomplished and experienced professional:

How do you invest in your professional knowledge? This question is a great way to gauge the prospective advisor's commitment to staying current on new laws, tax code changes, and cutting-edge ideas to help preserve and grow your wealth.

Ask about their recognized financial designations. Education is an important ingredient in selecting a financial advisor. An educated financial advisor will usually have at least one of the following credentials:

- CPA (Certified Public Accountant)
- CFP (Certified Financial Planner)
- ChFC (Chartered Financial Consultant)
- CLU (Chartered Life Underwriter)
- RFC (Registered Financial Consultant)

- APFS (Accredited Personal Financial Specialist)

The above organizations require that the professional pass an initial exam and obtain continuing professional education. By seeking a planner or advisor with one or more of the above designations, you can be reasonably assured that the planner has made a commitment to obtain sufficient knowledge to excel in financial planning and consulting.

STEP 10: BE SMART AND TRUST YOUR FEELINGS.

I'd love to tell you that our experience has taught us that as human beings, we will make decisions based entirely on logic. But I can't. People are not wired that way.

We've all been taught to never judge a book by its cover, right? But that is exactly what we often do. It's okay to be attracted to professionals with well-designed materials. That shows pride. Often, the ones who appear to be the best really are!

Then, when you meet face-to-face, gauge your emotions. If you feel comfort and a sense of greater security, then trust that feeling. Bring all the decision makers in your family to meet the advisory team. If you all feel that the advice given was in line with their published message and you all have more peace of mind at the conclusion of the meeting, then you've found yourself a good advisory team.

GLOSSARY
OF TERMS

Is there a field with more mumbo jumbo jargon than finance? Although our goal is to use plain English whenever possible, we know achieving that 100 percent of the time is impossible. Please see our list of terms used throughout this book with helpful definitions below.

PLAIN ENGLISH TRANSLATIONS

AGNOSTIC VIEW

In relation to your finances, this refers to keeping an open mind to all possible resources and solutions rather than holding a bias against any investment, offering, or strategy.

ANNUITY

Possibly the most confusing term in all of finance. This is because there are so many variations and uses for annuities. When discussing or considering annuities, make sure you have a clear understanding of what type you're discussing and its purpose.

ASSET-LIABILITY MATCHING

Trying to project the timing of cash or income needs and then making sure your money is available at that time.

BLINDERS STRATEGY

Super Retirement Planner's term for approaching your retirement savings when you are still decades away: begin saving automatically as soon as possible, set up your allocation, and forget about it!

BONDS

A loan to a corporation or the government.

CD

A certificate of deposit is offered by banks and credit unions and provides a set interest rate in exchange for a time commitment.

DYNAMIC REBALANCING

Rebalancing refers to ensuring the allocation of your nest egg is in line with your preferences. This is important, as your various savings and investments will not all earn the same returns. So over time, they will become out of balance.

Dynamic rebalancing refers to adjusting based on market conditions. For example, if stock market values are historically high, you might shift a portion of your allocation away from the stock market.

ENDOWMENT

A nonprofit institution's investable assets. Most are designed to keep the principal intact while using investment income for charitable purposes.

FEDERALLY BACKED US BONDS, NOTES, AND BILLS

When placing money into these, you are essentially loaning money to the federal government. These are considered risk-free because they receive the full faith and credit of the federal government.

FOUNDATION

An investment that provides principal and/or income guarantees.

GUARANTEED RETIREMENT INCOME PERCENTAGE (GRIP)

The percentage of your retirement income that has a guarantee backing it. Generally, the sources of retirement income that are considered to qualify would be Social Security, a pension, or a lifetime-income guaranteed annuity.

HUMAN CAPITAL

Your economic value, or your ability to earn money. Your human capital is highest when you are young and decreases to zero when you are no longer able to work.

INFLATION RISK

The risk that inflation will reduce your purchasing power in the future, either because inflation was higher than expected or inflation outpaced your investments.

LIABILITY MATCHING PORTFOLIO (LMP)

A way of setting aside part of your nest egg specifically for the intent of creating retirement income.

LONGEVITY RISK

The risk of outliving your nest egg, which is the number one retirement fear of Americans.[33]

MODERN PORTFOLIO THEORY

A theory on how investors can seek as much return as possible while taking as little risk as possible.

MUTUAL FUND

A pool of money collected from many investors to invest in stocks, bonds, or other assets.

PRIVATE EQUITY

Similar to stocks (see below). However, the ownership is of a company that is not public.

REAL ASSETS

Physical assets that have value. Common examples are real estate, metals, commodities, natural resources, and equipment.

---

33 https://www.journalofaccountancy.com/news/2016/oct/americans-fear-running-out-of-retirement-money-201615242.html.

REAL RETURN

This is the rate of return on your savings or investment *after* inflation. If you earn 5 percent interest and inflation is 3 percent, your real return is 2 percent.

RISK TOLERANCE

Refers to how much variance (up and down) you are comfortable with in your nest egg. Your risk tolerance can (and should!) change throughout your lifetime. Markets with significant downturns may make you realize that your tolerance isn't what you thought it was. These are important times to reevaluate.

ROOF

Any investment whose value changes at least daily due to fluctuations of the economy and/or markets.

SECURED PRIVATE DEBT

Debt refers to lending money (see BONDS). Private refers to dealing with a company that is not public. Secured means the loan is backed by collateral. So secured private debt is when you lend money to a private company that backs the loan with collateral.

Describes the risk that a retiree has of needing to draw from their accumulated retirement portfolios under volatile market conditions. If a retiree relies heavily on roof solutions, significant losses value just before or early in retirement could cause the nest egg balance to drop very quickly. This could ultimately require the retiree to either reduce spending or risk running out of money much more quickly than expected.

The percentage of your nest egg you are withdrawing to support your retirement lifestyle.

STOCKS

Ownership of a corporation. If you buy a share of stock in a company, you now own a tiny sliver of that corporation. If that company is public, the stock price fluctuates throughout the day.

UNCORRELATED ASSETS

Assets that react differently. Using these can provide tremendous diversification for your nest egg. You don't want all of your eggs in one basket, and you also want your baskets to be different from each other!

VOLATILITY RISK

The risk that a stock market downturn during retirement will require you to draw down your nest egg too quickly and potentially cause you to outlive your money.

WALLS

Nonguaranteed investments that generally avoid price volatility due to fluctuations of the economy and/or markets. These investments often seek steady monthly income and inflation protection while being asset-backed.

ACKNOWLEDGMENTS

Writing this book was more difficult than I expected and more rewarding than I could have ever imagined. None of this would have been possible without my wife, Janelle. Thank you for understanding my passion for the work we do with our clients as well as sharing our most important ideas through this book.

Thank you to my parents, Stephen and Madeleine Strubbe, for always prioritizing education, including English and writing, when I thought I would never use it in the future, and thank you for supporting me through college as well as in my decision to enter financial planning as my career.

Completing this required an all-star team at my office. Thank you to everyone at Preservation Specialists, LLC, including Linda Young, who, over her many years with us, has been instrumental in helping me find my voice.

Thank you to everyone who was part of taking this from idea to published book, including my project manager, Emily Anderson, the illustrator of the three Blueprint Mentors, Karina Acosta, and Lois Tuffin for helping me express my ideas.

Finally, I'm so thankful for my friends at Russell Total Wealth & Wellness, Rob Russell, Ron Russell, and Curv Miller, who were the original creators of the idea of divvying up between the Foundation, Walls, and Roof. Thank you so much for your generosity to allow so many other financial planners to use your concept to help their clients better understand their finances and, of course, to allow me to use this idea as the central idea of this book.

ABOUT THE AUTHOR

For over twenty years, Pat has taught retirees and pre-retirees how to preserve their assets and increase their income.

His own family's struggles influenced Pat to enter financial services. Pat vividly remembers being in high school when his grandfather needed nursing care. His mom had to handle the bills and coordinate payments, while his grandfather had to depend on someone else to take care of him, both physically and financially. The situation wore down his entire family. Today, Pat hopes to help others avoid the problems his family faced by showing them how to be proactive with their money.

Pat is a recurring guest on the WIS-TV (NBC) news with anchor Dawndy Mercer Plank. He was the financial columnist for the *Lexington Chronicle* for many years and has been featured in *USA Today*, *Columbia Business Monthly*, *Investor's Business Daily*, and other national publications, as well as on numerous radio shows around the country for his knowledge in the field of financial planning. Pat is a Chartered Financial

Consultant (ChFC®), Chartered Life Underwriter (CLU®), and Registered Financial Consultant (RFC®).

You can listen to Pat host the radio show *Save Your Retirement®* on WVOC-AM. He is also the author of the book *Save Your Retirement from Mass Destruction by the 7 Retirement Villains!*

Pat lives in Columbia, South Carolina, with his beautiful wife, Janelle. He is the proud father of four children: Carter, Ava, Gabriella, and Isla. Pat enjoys watching NBA basketball games with his friends and family. He loves to see his favorite team, the LA Lakers, whenever he can. An active member of Hope Lutheran Church in Irmo, Pat has served as an elder of finances since 2003.